Motivational Methods for Vegan Advocacy:
A Clinical Psychology Perspective

Casey T. Taft, PhD

Motivational Methods for Vegan Advocacy: A Clinical Psychology Perspective
Copyright © 2016 Casey T. Taft, PhD
All rights reserved.

Published by:
Vegan Publishers
Danvers, MA
www.veganpublishers.com

Cover artwork by Kara Maria Schunk
Cover and text design by Nicola May Design

Printed in the United States of America

ISBN: 978-1-940184-28-9

CONTENTS

CHAPTER 1

INTRODUCTION

The heart and soul of the animal advocacy movement is currently up for grabs. There has been a push on the part of the large, well-funded animal advocacy groups to promote vegetarianism rather than veganism, the reduction of animal consumption rather than an end to animal use, and a move away from the concept of animal use and abuse as an issue of social justice. These large groups and their supporters claim that this philosophy is what is most "effective" for preventing harm to animals and that this approach is based on scientific evidence and theory for how to bring about behavior change. As an expert in behavioral change, it was primarily this reason why I felt I needed to write this book. In fact, these notions could not be any farther from the truth. As I will be discussing throughout this book, promoting anything less than veganism will likely lead to individuals doing more harm to animals both in the short-term and the long-term, and it will validate the societal norm that animals are ours to use, perpetuating an atmosphere that prevents greater social change. A true behavioral change approach would necessitate promotion of a clear vegan end goal and the treatment of animal use as a fundamental issue of social justice, with the use of clear and supportive communication to facilitate motivation for change. I cannot sit back and witness the misuse of science and the language of behavioral change to justify advocacy that hurts the movement.

If we want to influence other people's behavior, we should consult with clinical psychology, since this discipline is tasked with creating lasting behavioral change. I feel compelled to offer insights and skills developed through my own clinical psychology background because I have been struck by how mainstream animal advocacy so often disregards basic principles of behavioral change that we psychologists take for granted. This book aims to bring a motivational behavioral change perspective to the animal advocacy community.

While there have been books written on the potential applicability of social psychology and marketing research to animal advocacy,[1, 2] which can help give us some insight into how interpersonal persuasion may work if applied to animal advocacy in a valid manner, these disciplines are not primarily concerned with how to produce clinically significant, long-term behavioral change of harmful behaviors. Marketing and strategies based on social psychology focus on provoking immediate change by manipulating the audience, whereas the discipline of clinical psychology focuses on how we can best change one's worldview, which is truly necessary to bring about the kinds of internal and behavioral changes that are essential for impactful animal advocacy. It would behoove us to look more to clinical psychology, a discipline with a long history of clinical development and applied research, to really understand how an individual undergoes internal and long-term change, and to better help others make changes that lead to reductions in animal suffering.

Since behavioral change experts have not been brought into the mainstream animal advocacy movement, I hope to reach out directly to activists and those within the advocacy community so that I may offer this perspective. My hope is that you will take away insights that will enhance your advocacy efforts and ultimately benefit animals.

Given the settings in which animal advocacy occurs—in one-on-one interactions with loved ones and strangers, on social media and other forms of personal communication, via direct action attempts to bring attention to these important issues, and through vegan education attempts—the skills, methods, and interventions used by clinical psychologists would have great value for activists. Naturally, being an effective and assertive communicator, learning how to work with those who are resistant to your change efforts, knowing how to best make your point, and moving someone along the path to behavioral change are critically important to promoting justice for animals.

We are the social change agents, and ending animal use for food, clothing, entertainment, and other purposes is up to all of us. It is doubtful that beings from outer space will be beaming down to earth to end the massive suffering inflicted upon nonhuman animals here. We are the ones who will have to figure this all out, which means that we need to find better ways to influence others to go vegan and end their exploitation of animals. In all of the settings for which we may have an influence on others, having an understanding of simple concepts and tools used to help others change problematic behaviors can only help us move closer towards our goal of achieving a vegan world.

I have been working clinically with men who engage in domestic violence for many years, and have been developing and evaluating anti-violence programs. I have a successful career as a leading authority on ending intimate partner violence in the most "treatment resistant" populations, and group therapy programs that I have developed are being implemented in healthcare systems across the country. I've seen thousands of violent, angry patients who come to me with no intention of changing and who resent me for even suggesting that their behavior is problematic. Most are court ordered to see me, so they're not asking for help. They engage in many of the same types of justifications that we vegan advocates encounter when interacting with non-vegans: minimization of the impacts of the violence, refusal to take personal responsibility, and the extreme hostility that often results from guilt and shame over one's actions.

Although the behaviors of violence towards relationship partners and the support of violence towards animals are distinctly different, the processes we use to work with these individuals to change their behavior bear many similarities. I have found that my work with violent perpetrators is critical in shaping my animal advocacy efforts as the co-owner of Vegan Publishers, a vegan-themed publishing company, and manager of our Facebook platform with over two hundred thousand followers, and I have observed many non-vegans go vegan as a result of these interactions, as I will illustrate with adapted real-life examples throughout this book.

If you tell an unmotivated person that their violent behaviors need to change—whether it's anger and abusive behavior towards an intimate partner or the support of needless violence towards animals—you will likely receive a defensive, hostile response. I have spent my career determining how best to manage that resistance and instead bring about positive behavioral change and the cessation of violence in spite of these obstacles. I have conducted randomized, controlled clinical trials (the "gold standard" of demonstrating effectiveness with regard to clinical intervention) with domestically violent men that demonstrate the efficacy of my approach. No such rigorous scientific work has yet been conducted determining the effectiveness of animal advocacy techniques.

I will be discussing some basic concepts as succinctly as possible. I will attempt to boil clinical psychology concepts and strategies down into a small number of critical elements that I hope people can learn from and use to develop new tools for animal advocacy. Hopefully much of what I write in this book will seem obvious to you—that usually means it is hitting on some truth. When concepts and strategies become overly complicated, they lose their meaning and impact. If reading this book empowers you with a new idea or concept that positively enhances your vegan advocacy, I will consider that a success.

This book is by no means exhaustive and it emphasizes how to improve our interactions with others to promote an end to animal use. I focus on vegan education efforts and how best to encourage others to go vegan because this is what is needed if we want to end demand for animal products and truly see an end to animal exploitation. There are other forms of animal advocacy that are also extremely valuable that I don't discuss, such as work done at animal sanctuaries to not only take in those nonhuman animals who are used and abused, but also to engage in vegan education and provide positive, hopeful examples amid so much animal abuse. I will focus on what I know best here: how to help convince others to end their unnecessary violence or contributions to violence.

In addition to my clinical training and expertise in enhancing motivation for change in those who engage in unnecessary violence, principles of abolitionist veganism[3, 4] have been influential in my thinking and dovetail with what I know about how to best help change behavior. Regardless of one's personal views about Gary Francione, the founder of the abolitionist movement, this perspective can serve as the foundation for powerful animal advocacy, particularly if approached from a motivational perspective that I will be discussing throughout this book. I tend to not label myself with any particular school of thought in clinical psychology or animal advocacy, however, because it is likely that I will write or say something that may not be entirely in keeping with a particular approach. Moreover, I am always learning more about how to be a better advocate and my views are continuously evolving. My hope is that readers will also develop and question their theoretical framework for understanding animal advocacy and will always strive to learn more and update their approaches. I recommend that every activist learn as much as they can about various approaches to inform their own advocacy, rather than follow any school of thought uncritically. My hope is that regardless of your particular perspective, you will find something of value in this book. By no means does one need to share my animal advocacy views to find something that they might resonate with or find useful.

Clinical psychology has much to offer the realm of animal advocacy, though I acknowledge that animal advocates are not all going to behave like clinical psychologists. I don't think anybody would want that! There are some things that I would say and do as an animal advocate that I would never do in my psychologist role. For example, psychologists tend to keep self-disclosure to a minimum, but in our animal advocacy it can be enormously helpful to tell our own vegan stories and use our own examples to convey a vegan message.

In the sections that follow, I first discuss considerations of social justice when trying to promote change and the importance of the language that we use in our advocacy. I then review what the science tells us about "effective animal advocacy." I next describe barriers for change in non-vegans and the importance of developing true long-term goals. Then I explain the importance of relationship building and assertive communication in bringing about change. A widely used theoretical model for helping others change problematic behaviors will then be covered. I then discuss advocacy traps to avoid, the importance of understanding linked oppressions, considerations of trauma in animal advocacy, and how best to communicate with non-vegan friends and loved ones. Finally, I discuss other therapeutic factors in animal advocacy and attempt to bring it all together, providing overarching suggestions for enhancing our advocacy. Throughout the book, I will endeavor to provide case examples that illustrate concepts and advocacy approaches that I feel are important.

CHAPTER 2

PROMOTING CHANGE IN THE CONTEXT OF SOCIAL JUSTICE

We must recognize that encouraging others to end their use of animals is not the same thing as suggesting others engage in other forms of behavioral change, such as increasing exercise, for example. This is because there are direct victims in the former and not in the latter. Therefore, any approach that we take in helping others go vegan must appreciate the social justice dimensions of the issue, since others are experiencing oppression and injustice as a result of the behaviors we are trying to help change.

Unfortunately, what it really means to be vegan is not well-understood, as popular culture and mainstream animal advocacy organizations promote the view that veganism is simply a diet. In fact, the concept of veganism originally put forward by The Vegan Society was always about ethics and minimizing the harm we do to nonhuman animals in all ways possible and practical.[1] The definition of veganism described by Leslie J. Cross in 1949 involved "the principle of the emancipation of animals from exploitation by man." The definition was later modified: "to seek an end to the use of animals by man for food, commodities, work, hunting, vivisection, and by all other uses involving exploitation of animal life by man." When The Vegan Society became a registered charity in 1979, it was further refined as follows:

A philosophy and way of living which seeks to exclude—as far as is possible and practicable—all forms of exploitation of, and cruelty to, animals for food, clothing or any other purpose; and by extension, promotes the development and use of animal-free alternatives for the benefit of humans, animals and the environment.

Throughout this book, I will discuss how it should never be acceptable to promote the view that it is okay to simply reduce our animal consumption; only veganism (*ending* our animal use) is ethically defensible. Being vegan is the minimum we should do if we truly acknowledge that our use of animals is a social justice issue.[2] When we encourage others to go vegan, many will of course cut down on their animal consumption on their way to veganism, such that promoting veganism leads to both incremental and long-term change. However, we ought not suggest that to simply reduce rather than end our own contribution to animal exploitation is a worthy end goal.

The larger animal advocacy organizations have taken the approach of promoting vegetarianism and a reduction in animal consumption, rather than emphasizing veganism as a goal for all to strive for, and I believe this is a profound mistake on three grounds: (1) it fails to challenge the entrenched social norms supporting our use and abuse of animals, (2) there is no empirical evidence that this "reducetarian"[3,4] approach is more effective for promoting either incremental or long-term change, and (3) this approach that fails to promote a vegan end goal runs counter to what we know about enhancing motivation for true behavioral change and the importance of setting long-term end goals in our change efforts. Much of what I discuss in this book focuses on this final point.

For every social justice movement that has led to great change, those at the forefront were able to change the way that we see certain oppressed groups, such as women, people of color, non-straight people, trans people, and so on. The same is needed for animal advocacy and a shift towards veganism; we will never be able to shift the paradigm for animals if we continue to go along with the oppressive notion that we can ethically do harm to animals in moderation.

To examine whether we're treating our animal use as a social justice issue, all we need to do is to hypothetically place an oppressed human group in the place of nonhuman animals. For example, would we ever promote only a reduction in racism, or a "baby steps" approach to ending racism rather than demanding a complete end to racist practices? Would we encourage those who engage in domestic violence to merely reduce their physical violence towards their partners, or would we demand that society refuses to condone any intimate partner violence? No, we would not actively promote a simple reduction in oppression for any group of humans, and nor should we actively encourage only moderate oppression of nonhuman animals. The only reason that some are able to get away with advocating for a reduction in animal use and abuse is "speciesism," or the damaging belief that some animals are "higher" than others.

While individual advocates may not think of themselves as speciesists, they promote a speciesist paradigm when they convey acceptance of any nonhuman animal abuse that would never, under any circumstances, be considered acceptable if human animals were those experiencing the injustice. Moreover, while the individual advocate would argue that they don't believe that any animal use in moderation is acceptable, they must recognize that when they ask others to only reduce their animal consumption they are giving the message that some animal use is in fact acceptable, thus condoning violence towards animals.

The nonhuman animals we are fighting to help deserve nothing less than a complete rejection of their use by those who claim to be advocating for them. When we give the impression that it's ethically acceptable to do harm to animals in moderation, or that we reduce their abuse over time, we are ourselves engaging in an injustice towards the animals. Having an unequivocal stance that veganism is a social justice issue doesn't mean that we are aggressive with others in our approach. On the contrary, we can and should promote veganism as a social justice issue while at the same time encouraging others to go vegan in a supportive, empathic, and motivational manner.

I often witness animal advocates bemoaning the fact that we do not have a more cohesive movement. The reality is that we have groups who view animal advocacy in entirely different ways and have completely different goals. One group sees our animal use as an issue of social justice and their goal is to help create a vegan world that does not tolerate any animal use. The other group downplays social justice and works to reduce animal use and improve animal welfare, with the belief that a vegan world is not a realistic goal, at least not for the foreseeable future. The difficulty in creating unity across these two groups is that the efforts of the latter group work directly against the efforts of the former. We will never have a vegan world if most animal advocates, and all of the larger advocacy organizations, promote the view that animals can continue to be harmed in moderation or "humanely."

My hope for the future of animal advocacy is that we all fight against the view that nonhuman animals can be bred and used for any purpose at all. The only way advocates can claim that reducing animal use, rather than ending animal use, is a worthy goal is if they believe that nonhuman animals should not have a basic right to their lives. Moreover, the focus on reducing exploitation ignores countless victims, including those who are still directly consumed, those who are used for their skin (e.g., leather and furs), those used in zoos and water parks, and those tested on for useless cosmetics testing and scientific experiments. What does promotion of a reducetarian ethic do for these animals to prevent their suffering and needless deaths? Only the promotion of veganism advocates for the end of all animal use for all purposes, and so we are much more inclusive and effective as advocates for *all* animals when we unequivocally state that veganism is the absolute least that we can do. With all of the great energy in the animal advocacy movement and so many people who want to help animals, if we would collectively focus our energies on educating others about veganism we would be sending out the consistent message that all forms of animal use must end and that all of this is an issue of social justice.

If all animal advocates and advocacy groups were to promote veganism as the least we can do for nonhuman animals—in other words as an issue of social justice that gives nonhuman animals a modicum of ethical consideration—we would begin to see a greater change in the way our larger society views animals. The only way that we can unite this movement and accelerate social change regarding our views and treatment of nonhuman animals is if we all get on board with viewing our use and abuse of animals as one of the critical social justice issues of our time. Therefore, we must reject a focus on dietary reductions of animal "products" that ignore the injustice of breeding and killing these creatures in the first place.

CHAPTER 3

LANGUAGE IS IMPORTANT

The language that we use in our advocacy is of critical importance and says a lot about how we view nonhuman animals and our role as animal advocates. When we engage in advocacy with non-vegans it is usually best to strive to avoid terms promoted by the animal agriculture industries that create a disconnection between the suffering of nonhuman animals and the packaged "product" that the consumer purchases at the store. Rather than referring to "meat," the expression "animal flesh" is a more apt descriptor. Rather than using "pork," "beef," or any other similar terms, it is best to call it what it actually is: the flesh from a pig or cow, etc. Rather than using the term "dairy," we might instead refer to "cows' milk." Language that we can use to highlight the reality that non-vegans consume once-sentient beings can only help us break down those walls that our culture has helped create, which hinders awareness about our collective animal use.

In her book *Vegan's Daily Companion*,[1] Colleen Patrick-Goudreau discusses how we can best communicate with others in a manner that affirms our ethical stance against animal use. We may encounter others who will ask us whether we "can" eat certain foods. The author suggested that we should respond to such questions by noting that we *can* in fact eat animals but we choose not to do so. By affirming that we are vegan by choice highlights that our veganism is not about dietary restrictions or willpower, but rather a moral imperative to prevent injustice towards nonhuman animals.

How we refer to ourselves and describe the goals of our advocacy also matters greatly. Mainstream advocacy groups have all moved away from promoting veganism as a moral imperative to promoting "vegetarianism" in their advocacy materials in response to survey research suggesting that the general public views vegetarianism as a more attainable goal than veganism.[2] The problem with this is that vegetarianism includes the consumption of animal "products," and the dairy industry involves as much or more suffering than the meat industry. It is unfathomable that those purporting to be leaders in animal advocacy would be giving the message to others that it is acceptable to continue to do harm to at least some animals as an end goal. Mind you, these materials and this message are not asking others to go vegetarian as a step towards veganism; it simply asks others to go vegetarian, which includes the direct exploitation of animals. As I will be discussing, this also does not make much sense from a goal-setting and behavioral change standpoint.

Some advocates avoid discussing "veganism" because some non-vegans may consider it a derogatory term. We should keep in mind that as with any social justice issue, there will always be those who vehemently disagree with the end goals and will therefore characterize supporters of the movement in various negative ways. One need only look at how feminists and black activists are portrayed as "angry" or "crazy," for examples. If we feel ashamed to call ourselves "vegan," we internalize the dialogue used by those who would like us to fail. This is the exact opposite of what we should be doing! We should be proud to call ourselves vegans and we should always emphasize that veganism is about justice and an end to animal exploitation.

There is no better word than "veganism" to describe what veganism actually means. The word conveys that it is a moral imperative to avoid doing harm to animals. I'm not aware of any other term that captures that same definition. When advocates ditch the word "vegan," their advocacy suffers from a lack of clarity in their communication to those whose behavior we most want to impact. We are more likely to be divided as a movement if some proudly wear the vegan label and others reject it. There are enough barriers that separate those who advocate for animals; how we describe ourselves need not be one of them.

The term "vegan police" gets thrown around a lot in animal advocacy circles and online. Vegans are often called "vegan police" by other animal advocates when they attempt to hold others accountable regarding their use of animals, educate others about what it means to be vegan, or question somebody else's use of animals in some manner. Most often, the term is used by those promoting something less than veganism as "good enough" for nonhuman animals. If we view animal advocacy as an issue of justice for animals, we should never be shamed for trying to promote veganism in any way. Rather than getting personally offended when someone is talking to us about how to avoid animal exploitation, it's always best to try to listen to what they're saying and engage in introspection regarding whether there's any validity to their comments. All too often, I have witnessed vegans and non-vegans alike immediately go into "defense mode" and reject any form of constructive feedback. When we stay constantly defensive, it prevents us from learning from others and from working to be better advocates.

Another expression used by some advocates to shame other advocates is "moral purity." This term is typically used to suggest that vegans should be careful not to appear too "extreme" in their vegan advocacy. In other words, those who criticize others for engaging in moral purity are telling us that we do not need to be completely consistent in our veganism. A scenario that is often described is one in which a vegan is out to dinner with non-vegan friends, and the vegan discovers that there is some animal ingredient that is mistakenly in their food. Some will argue that the vegan who refuses to eat that food is engaging in "moral purity," which will serve to reaffirm to the non-vegans that vegans are extreme zealots.

Again, we must be very careful not to silence ourselves, or to engage in behavior that is harmful to nonhuman animals, because others view the promotion of justice for all animals to be extreme. When we internalize the notion that vegans are extreme, or angry, we have quieted our own voices for animals and weakened our advocacy. Our behavior should not be guided by fear-based avoidance of speaking out against injustice. It is quite easy to maintain a clear vegan position while also showing others that we are fully rational, compassionate people. I provide a number of tips throughout this book about how we can communicate with others in an assertive yet compassionate manner.

Were we to see animal use as an issue of social justice, we would not criticize others for assertively speaking out for animals in any way, and we would not be more concerned for how others will perceive us than for the fate of animals who are needlessly killed. We will never turn someone away from veganism who otherwise would have gone vegan by being consistent with our vegan message, or by refusing to eat animal ingredients in a restaurant. We need to learn from each other and constantly strive to better speak out for animals, because if we don't, we all suffer the consequences.

The sad truth about mainstream animal advocacy and the largest advocacy groups is that they inform their advocacy decisions based on market research. In other words, when determining how best to encourage people to stop exploiting animals, they ask those doing the exploiting how we should craft our message to them. This is not something that happens with any other social justice movement, and nor should it. Do you think the Black Lives Matter folks conduct surveys with white racists in an effort to determine how we can end racial injustice? Do feminists conduct focus groups with sexist men about how we can best end patriarchy and violence against women? Of course not! It is absurd to ask those doing the oppressing how we should talk to them to encourage them to stop the oppression.

Of course, when we ask a non-vegan how we should engage in advocacy, they will tell us that we should only ask them to cut down on eating animal "products." They would prefer that we never mentioned the word "vegan" at all because it makes them uncomfortable. We should not stop short of asking others to go vegan by suggesting that they go vegetarian or reducetarian instead because it makes them more comfortable. Being comfortable does not bring about the radical shift that we need for animals. We need to help the broader society step out of its comfort zone and ultimately reject the injustice we expose animals to in our use and abuse of them. Nonhuman animals deserve justice and an end to their use, not market researchers who are asking those engaging in the injustice how we can best talk to them. Our movement should not be guided by the preferences of those who never want to see the end of animal exploitation.

Changing our language in response to possible derogatory uses and negative perceptions is reactionary, leading to apologist attitudes and inauthenticity. As advocates, it is critically important to base our approach on what is truthful, morally right, and personally authentic. We will not be successful in convincing others to stop contributing to the harm of nonhuman animals if we refuse to be honest with them. Clinical psychologists have long known that when we are less than open and honest with those whom we are working with, we will be less able to align with them and help bring about true internal change. If we believe that others should go vegan, we should talk to them about veganism. We need to give others more credit to be able to listen to a clear vegan message and determine for themselves if they wish to bring their behavior in line with their values when it comes to the treatment of nonhuman animals.

CHAPTER 4

WHAT DOES THE SCIENCE TELL US ABOUT EFFECTIVE ANIMAL ADVOCACY?

There has been great misuse of the term "effective" as it is applied to animal advocacy. There seem to be attempts made by the larger, mainstream animal advocacy groups and many individual advocates to claim that their approach is "evidence based." Typically the approaches being advocated for are those that fail to promote veganism and refuse to view veganism as an issue of social justice. This is highly misleading and unfortunate because there really is no evidence that any one approach is any more effective than another in producing either short-term or long-term behavioral change or reductions in animal suffering, and those who don't regularly consume research are being misled to engage in animal advocacy that may ultimately be doing the animals more harm than good.

I have witnessed a new cottage industry of advocacy research seeking effective approaches for helping animals. While this is a worthy goal, these groups are conducting and promoting flawed, pseudoscientific research that doesn't really tell us anything about effective animal advocacy. Data from this research are being used by Animal Charity Evaluators (ACE) to determine the most "worthy" charities to donate to, which is problematic because we end up with a "garbage in / garbage out" scenario where flawed data are input to generate flawed recommendations. Unfortunately, ACE regularly rates the organizations conducting this research as top charities, and ACE top charities are overwhelmingly (perhaps exclusively) professionalized organizations that do not promote veganism as a moral imperative, which has contributed to questions about bias in their rating system.[1]

As an example of flawed pseudoscientific work, Faunalytics (formerly the Humane Research Council) conducted a highly publicized study survey[2] of over eleven thousand respondents to better understand factors that lead to the long-term adoption of a "vegan" or vegetarian diet. For purposes of statistical analyses, "vegans" (defined as those adopting a plant-based diet) and vegetarians were grouped together. A key finding was that there was more than five times the number of former vegetarians/vegans than current vegetarians/vegans, suggesting that adherence to such diets is low and problematic. Based on a series of analyses comparing current versus former vegans/vegetarians, the authors drew several conclusions including that we should place greater emphasis on reductions in animal consumption relative to complete cessation (reducetarianism) and that we should focus more on the "how" of vegetarianism/veganism (presumably relative to the "why" of going vegan).

A glaring problem with these conclusions is that they ran counter to what the data actually showed. The most important variables that determined whether one remained a vegan/vegetarian was whether they maintained their diet for reasons related to animal rights, environmental rights, or social justice. More specifically, those indicating that they followed a vegan/vegetarian diet due to "animal protection," "feelings of disgust about meat/animal products," "concern for the environment," and "social justice or world hunger" were most likely to continue with their meat-free diet.

A separate analysis showed that the primary challenge to maintaining a meat-free diet among study participants was that they didn't see vegetarianism/veganism as part of their identity, suggesting that when one internalizes an ethic to end animal use, they will remain vegan or vegetarian. Across each of these sets of analyses, variables that refer to *empathy* for others were more strongly linked to continued adherence to a meat-free diet than self-interested concerns such as health, cost, taste, social influence, religious/spiritual beliefs, trendiness, or cravings. When we do it for other animals, we are less likely to revert back to consuming animal products.

In other words, the actual data suggested that we should promote veganism according to its original definition of minimizing harm to others. And we should empower people to proudly identify with being vegan and unashamedly eliminate animal products from their lives. In sum, the results suggest that we should be placing greater focus on the "why" of veganism (the ethical case), place more emphasis on encouraging others to end all harm done to other animals (not reducing meat intake), and work to increase identification with veganism (not weaken it). The data provide us with a story that is the exact opposite of what the researchers were telling us the data were saying. Their conclusions appeared to be biased to further their own view of advocacy, which is dangerous because many in the media and animal advocacy world simply went with the misinterpretations of the authors when they discussed this study and shared them on their social media pages.

This was only one obvious problem with this study. Other deviations from the accepted scientific method were:

1. They did not generate a set of testable hypotheses that were based on a specific theory or conceptual model. If a study does not have any expectations for what the data analysis will tell us, then hypotheses can't be tested and the study should be considered exploratory.

2. They did not operationally define and measure the constructs of interest in a clear manner using accepted definitions. For example, "veganism" was mischaracterized as simply a diet when veganism is an ethic that goes far beyond diet, and vegans and vegetarians were grouped together in data analyses despite obvious differences between these groups.

3. The authors went far beyond the evidence in their interpretations.

4. The authors did not subject the research to a peer review process such that other experts in the field could offer their input and ensure that the research was scientifically sound and unbiased. This is no small point. For some reason, in the animal advocacy realm, many seem to think that it's acceptable to conduct a research study on their own and then throw their findings up on their website or in a press release, completely bypassing the peer review process that is the bedrock of all truly scientific endeavors.

Another notable, highly publicized example is a recent study by Humane League Labs.[3] They administered booklets that "discussed the cruelty of factory farming and the health benefit of removing animal products from one's diet." Next, the authors used eight different booklets that made different requests—some asking readers to "eat vegan," some asking readers to "eat vegetarian," some encouraging readers to "eat less meat," and some encouraging readers to "cut out or cut back on" meat and other animal products.

Once again, a major overarching problem with this research is that veganism was not properly represented. A vegan messaging approach would not only focus on "factory farming" but would discuss the ethics of using animals in all ways. It would also not focus on health. So again, if the authors are going to make any inferences about vegan messaging and its effectiveness, then truly vegan messaging should be employed.

There were major scientific issues with this research, such as a low response rate and a lot of missing data, unequal group sizes and failure to randomize participants to group, etc. What is far more concerning, however, is how the data were again misinterpreted in a manner consistent with the worldview of this group. Those in the "control" condition reduced their meat and dairy consumption more than any other group. Moreover, the only statistically significant findings demonstrated that those in the control condition reduced their consumption more than those who received different messages.

In other words, the only "meaningful" finding from the main data analyses was that individuals reduced their meat and dairy consumption more when they were not asked to change anything than when they are asked to make some kind of change in their consumption. In any research study, when those in a control condition who do not receive an intervention evidence better outcomes (meat and dairy reduction) than those who receive an intervention (different requests), the only conclusion that can be drawn is that the intervention(s) didn't work.

The authors, on the other hand, have interpreted results that were not statistically significant to conclude that the message to "cut out or cut back on" meat and other animal products "might be the most effective approach" to get people to reduce animal product consumption. These conclusions are unwarranted given the actual findings, the lack of statistical significance of differences between groups (except for differences showing those receiving no message decreased consumption the most), and the methodological issues that call into question the validity of the data.

My intention is not to pick on these groups for conducting this pseudoscientific work. Indeed, I have yet to see one animal advocacy study that conforms to these elements of the scientific method delineated above. As one might expect, those conducting this research have not appreciated it when I've called their work "pseudoscience." I get no joy and receive no benefit from criticizing the work of those in animal advocacy. Frankly, I abhor having to review other people's research because I have to do it so often in my day job. It's excruciating for me to have to read the details of a flawed research study in an effort to determine if the work has scientific merit. But when I witness such blatantly biased work that fails to conform to what I know as a credible scientific method, I feel compelled to review the work and help inform the vegan public about the misuse of science and the resulting misleading implications that can derail our movement.

Pseudoscience is "a claim, belief, or practice that is presented as scientific, but does not adhere to a valid scientific methodology, lacks supporting evidence or plausibility, cannot be reliably tested, or otherwise lacks scientific status."[4] When a group frames a study and misinterprets flawed results to fit their preferred mode of advocacy, they are engaging in pseudoscience. Such practices appear to be all too common in the animal advocacy realm, which is disappointing and potentially dangerous. The media and other groups report the conclusions from this research assuming it is valid. The organizations that conduct this kind of work can falsely claim that their form of advocacy is "evidence based." It is potentially harmful to animals for people to promote the notion of one form of advocacy as more effective than another based on flawed and seriously biased research. We can and must do better than this.

Others have asked me what my thoughts were about the work of Nick Cooney, Director of Education at Mercy for Animals, who has applied findings primarily from social psychology and marketing science to animal advocacy in his writings[5, 6] and professional speaking events. This work is often cited as evidence that the promotion of veganism is not "effective" for most people. For example, he has discussed how the "Foot-in-the-Door Technique,"[7] shown to be an effective sales technique, might apply to animal advocacy. The idea is that rather than making a large request, such as asking the person to go vegan, it may be best to ask for a small request, such as to reduce meat consumption, and that when they acquiesce to this request they will be more likely to accept subsequent requests.

There is simply no actual research demonstrating that this approach, asking others to "cut down on" animal use, is any more effective than asking others to go vegan according to any metric, and I do not believe that this incremental approach can be effective, for reasons I discuss throughout this book. Although presumably well-intentioned, Mr. Cooney and other animal advocates make large leaps in the way they have applied marketing research and social psychology findings focused on one particular area of behavior change to the realm of animal advocacy. If foot-in-the-door helps some people become more aware of their home energy use, for example, this really tells us nothing about whether this approach would help others go vegan, because energy use and violence towards nonhuman animals are not even close to being similar forms of problem behavior. Again, we can't rely on speculation and distortions of the application of theory to demonstrate that "science" is on our side; that is anti-scientific. We can discuss the possible relevance of such techniques, but we should not claim that there is evidence of effectiveness in animal advocacy.

Moreover, salesmanship techniques and gimmicky strategies taken from social psychology experiments lacking in generalizability to animal advocacy are not going to produce the change that we need to see across individuals or in the larger society. For long-standing problematic behaviors for which individuals are highly resistant to change, we need more robust techniques that are based on stronger theories of true internal behavioral change. We will not trick others into going vegan. We need to find ways to bring about real change, taking into consideration existing values and beliefs, recognizing the barriers for them changing their behavior, and using communication strategies that help build relationships and move people further along in recognizing a need to change behavior.

As I will be discussing further, there are several very promising directions for us to go in enhancing our advocacy. I will be discussing some of the most powerful strategies used in clinical psychology to bring about behavioral change even in the most resistant individuals. Setting effective long-term goals, recognizing the place along the continuum of readiness for change that a person currently resides and using motivational strategies, working with them collaboratively to help them change their behavior, recognizing key core themes or schemas that may be at the heart of their use of animals, and following a trauma-informed perspective are literally some of the most powerful tools that behavioral change agents use. These strategies are also universal in that they can be applied to any behavioral problem. I am perpetually surprised that there has heretofore not been an effort to apply these strategies to animal advocacy or vegan messaging.

Even if—and this is a big if—a well-conducted, randomized, controlled trial suggested that giving others the message that reducing animal use was more strongly associated with short-term animal use reduction than giving others the message to go vegan, I still would not support this "reducetarian" approach. This is because it waters down our collective message of justice for animals and does great harm in the long-term if it hinders our ability to change the paradigm regarding the use of animals in our society. Moreover, long-term animal consumption is more important than short-term incremental changes because if one goes vegan, it means that they minimize the harm they do to animals over the course of many years. There are basic limitations of science that would make it very difficult to conduct credible research that truly examined the long-term impacts of different forms of advocacy because what is ultimately the greatest outcome we can have is to create new vegans and to change the way that nonhuman animals are perceived in our society, and research designs examining these long-term outcomes focused on the individual and society would have limitations as to what they could truly tell us.

Despite these limitations of our current scientific methods, we can learn much more about what helps create behavioral change if we employ experts trained to do this kind of research and use accepted scientific methods. The "gold standard" in the field of clinical psychology is the conduct of randomized controlled trials. At a minimum, outcome variables should be clearly and appropriately defined and measured, participants should be randomly assigned to distinct intervention groups, those conducting the assessments should be "blind" to treatment condition (i.e., they should conduct the assessments without the knowledge of which group they're assigned to), independent monitors should determine whether the interventions delivered are consistent with the stated approaches, the data should be analyzed by an unbiased expert using standard statistical approaches designed specifically to examine change over time, the findings should be interpreted in an unbiased manner, and the final manuscript should be submitted for peer review at a scientific journal by other independent reviewers (who typically don't have access to the author names).

It would certainly be easier if we could avoid having to follow the scientific method, but if we're going to participate in science, and suggest that some interventions are more effective than others, we need to follow certain standards for it to have any meaning at all. Otherwise, there is the potential for putting out false information that can be misleading and that divert scarce resources to the wrong places.

I have spent the past eight years of my clinical research career as Principal Investigator of multi-million-dollar, large-scale randomized controlled trials funded by the Centers for Disease Control and Department of Defense, and have also been conducting implementation research showing that my programs work in real-world settings.[8, 9] The reason I did this work was because I wanted to develop an "evidence-based" intervention to prevent and end intimate partner violence, and I wanted to change the paradigm for how we work with perpetrators of violence. Through this funded work, I have shown empirically that our trauma-informed anti-violence program is the first of its kind that is demonstrated to be effective. Without randomized controlled trials, we have no confidence that those in our programs end their violence more than those who attend other programs or who may end their violence on their own.

The same is true for animal advocacy. We really can't say anything about the "effectiveness" of one approach versus another if we don't demonstrate it through a randomized controlled trial. So we should not give the impression that our animal advocacy approach is somehow better than other approaches based on empirical evidence, because we could not possibly be any further from demonstrating superior efficacy of one approach versus another in animal advocacy.

CHAPTER 5

WHY DO PEOPLE CONTINUE TO LIVE NON-VEGAN?

If we hope to change others' behavior and bring about a large shift towards veganism, it can be helpful to think about how their non-vegan behaviors developed and what maintains them. Psychologists typically "diagnose" the problem(s) and the thoughts, feelings, and behaviors that support problematic behavior before developing a treatment strategy. Likewise, when we engage in animal advocacy, it is helpful to have an understanding of what gets in the way of change for the person we're communicating with.

Just like any problem behavior, consuming and using animals is obviously a learned behavior that can be unlearned. Almost all of us were raised to view animals as "things" for us to use, and we were taught that animals are "lesser" than humans — the very definition of speciesism. We were taught to love our pets, while we were routinely fed the bodies of farmed animals.[1] Many of us were taken to zoos or other venues where we saw animals used for entertainment, and animal exploitation was normalized in every way possible. Such powerful conditioning is difficult to unlearn. Many vegans will tell you that they did not realize how powerfully they'd been brainwashed until later in life. Even the most intelligent and aware activists often admit to being completely blinded to the exploitation of animals for the better part of their lives.

This powerful conditioning is typically how we have learned to exploit nonhuman animals, but what keeps the exploitation going even when there is so much information out there about how we are harming animals, the planet, and ourselves with our choices? There is no single factor that can explain the unwillingness of non-vegans to go vegan, and the possible reasons I describe below are certainly not an exhaustive list, but they touch on some factors that I believe play a role.

First, acknowledging our regular participation in the exploitation of animals requires some degree of self-reflection, which is likely to be uncomfortable for most people. Few people like to think of themselves as "animal exploiters." When one becomes aware of our collective mistreatment of animals, they will have to acknowledge that they are part of the problem and are contributing to the harming of animals. This can be difficult for some otherwise considerate and compassionate individuals to reconcile.

I have frequently seen non-vegans exhibit a classic shame response wherein they are presented with information regarding animal cruelty, then quickly turn to anger, which they direct at the messenger. Rather than undergoing the difficult process of developing awareness and insight into their own guilt and shame, and reflecting on their behaviors connected to that shame, they instead direct those feelings outward and present irrational justifications for their contributions to continued animal mistreatment. They may describe feeling "attacked" by the messenger of this new information even when no actual attack has occurred because they are experiencing shame and are battling their own "self talk" in which they may be unconsciously (or consciously) questioning their own morality. I know this all sounds very psychoanalytic, and that is not my intention (because I don't subscribe to that school of psychological thought), but it is undeniable that shame is a leading factor that hinders people from taking responsibility for problematic behavior and moving towards behavioral change.[2]

Second, myths about veganism abound, most of which are products of a time long gone by, when nutritional science viewed plant-based diets in a negative light despite little research on the topic. Many still espouse the false views that vegans have difficulty getting protein, need to take several supplements to be healthy, are all weak and sickly, don't care about humans, etc. Animal advocates have been barraged by such myths. As such, it's important to have a grasp of the facts and ethical arguments[3, 4] that dispel these myths as well as those that show the incredible health benefits of a plant-based diet.[5]

Third, in these difficult economic times, many people are focusing on survival and don't feel they can make significant lifestyle changes. If someone is having trouble paying the bills, or feeding their children, or is struggling with a host of other issues, they may not feel that it is the right time for them to focus on ending others' suffering. Unfortunately, there is also a common misperception that vegan diets are more expensive than non-vegan diets, and for those living in impoverished areas characterized by "food deserts," it may indeed be more difficult to find affordable vegan food.

As vegan advocates, we can acknowledge the personal challenges some may be experiencing and also use that dialogue to find solutions that may work for these individuals. We can highlight the long-term costs—ethically, medically, economically, and spiritually—of consuming animals. We can also promote the view that when we advocate for others, we feel better about ourselves. Doing good for others is an excellent way to combat depression and a host of adjustment problems, so periods when we are struggling may actually be the best time to go vegan.

Fourth, some people have an unhealthy relationship with food in general or may have developed rigid patterns. For example, some may have found that their animal-based diet has helped them maintain a particular physique they were working to achieve, and nothing anyone says about the benefits of veganism will convince them to consider changing. It may be more difficult to convince others to go vegan when their animal consumption is related to long-standing patterns or self-image issues, and we may need to provide them with accurate information and encourage them to explore these other problems through whatever means they think will be most helpful, such as seeing a vegan-friendly nutritionist or mental health expert.

A theoretical model that I have found key in my anti-violence work, and that undergirds the program that I have developed that has been shown to end intimate partner violence,[6] is the social information processing model.[7] This model states that we go through a series of cognitive steps when we are making sense of social information and choosing a course of action. The initial stage involves attempting to decode and interpret a particular situation and we then generate responses to the situation, choose a plan of action, execute a response, and respond to feedback after our response. A number of factors may influence how we interpret and respond to situations as we work through the states of social information processing, such as our learning histories, prior trauma, substance use, traumatic brain injuries, etc.

A good deal of research shows that those who engage in unnecessary violence exhibit deficits across the social information processing stages, especially the stage in which we are decoding or interpreting social situations.[8, 9, 10, 11] A violent individual is more likely than a nonviolent person to falsely assume that another person is being hostile to them or otherwise has negative intentions. Violent individuals are particularly likely to twist things in a negative direction and assume the worst of others.

In the context of needless animal use, similarly unclear or distorted thinking may creep in for one who is not able to recognize the harm they do to nonhuman animals. Because of our prior history and exposure to animal killing, we delude ourselves into thinking that this is normal and natural, and we fail to see the injustice that we inflict on these sentient beings. Prior history of trauma may also serve to inhibit our cognitive clarity and cause us to distort our worlds in a more hostile and violent direction, leading to greater violent behavior, as my own research has shown to be the case for military Veterans exposed to combat trauma and posttraumatic stress disorder.[12]

An important key to behavioral change is that we can be most helpful when we tailor our strategy to the stage the individual is in with respect to their motivational readiness. If the individual is having a difficult time coming to grips with their own animal exploitation, we should avoid making shaming statements and make it clear that we are not accusing them of being a "bad person." If the person espouses myths about veganism, we might present factual information that dispels them. If the individual is dealing with other personal issues, we might share how going vegan actually helped us feel much happier and healthier, and that they may experience the same benefits.

One of the most important questions that I ask those who express interest in going vegan but demonstrate some reluctance to commit is "What gets in the way of you going vegan?" This leaves the ball in their court, so to speak, and gives them the opportunity to let me know what is really getting in the way for them. They sometimes will say that they're ready to make the full change if only they can find a replacement for a specific animal-based food, or they may discuss how they only use animal products in the context of specific social situations, or they describe concerns about health and nutrition, etc. This allows me to introduce an important discussion about what I can do to help them overcome these perceived barriers that are often a product of their own thinking rather than something truly tangible and realistic. When we can help the individual work through these potential barriers and get to the point where they can see themselves as vegan, we have made great progress in helping to create another vegan.

Regardless of the reasons for non-veganism, we will not be successful in our advocacy if we accuse others of being "murderers," "rapists," or any other derogatory term, because this will only increase resistance and elicit a stronger shame/anger response. Rather, we should avoid labeling or stigmatizing others as we are attempting to help them change their behavior. We should also emphasize that we are not attacking them personally, but, rather, are advocating for animals and bringing attention to problematic behavior that most of us have engaged in at some point. We must do this while emphasizing the importance of a vegan end goal (Chapter 6), developing a positive relationship with the individual (Chapter 7), and maintaining a clear and assertive stance (Chapter 8). In Chapter 9, I discuss in greater detail how to meet the individual where they are in terms of their readiness to change.

CHAPTER 6

LONG-TERM GOAL SETTING

A wealth of research in the field of motivation demonstrates the importance of long-term goal setting.[1] Importantly, goals need not be easy to attain in the short-term. In fact, the underlying premise of the widely studied and empirically supported "Goal-setting Theory"[2, 3] is that specific and difficult goals lead to greater behavioral change. Moreover, this body of evidence indicates that when we simply ask others to "do their best," this leads to less behavioral change because it is difficult for one to engage in self-evaluation of their own change without a clear goal.[4]

Of course, one of the first things that any clinical psychologist will discuss with a new client during the initial visit is long-term goal setting. When working with violent clients, clinicians promote the end goal of being and remaining completely non-violent. A therapist would never set a long-term goal of ending only some violence, or ending only physical but not psychological violence. Once the primary long-term goal is stated, the client is then encouraged to come up with ways to achieve that long-term goal, such as better communication and tools and strategies for handling anger-provoking situations more effectively.

All of the large mainstream animal advocacy groups take great pains to reach out to non-vegans by enticing them with meatless alternatives, promoting "Meatless Monday" campaigns, cutting down on meat, etc., but they miss the most important component of any behavioral change strategy—a clearly defined end goal. It is surprising how rarely veganism is a stated goal in animal advocacy efforts. How can we expect people to go vegan on a large scale and minimize all forms of violence towards animals if it is rarely the objective of efforts intended to change behavior? We will have a very difficult time "tricking" people into going vegan by suggesting they cut down on meat or by offering tasty vegan food, and there is no evidence that this method is effective in effecting long-term, measurable change. If we want unnecessary violence towards animals to end and view that goal as a social justice issue, then veganism should be what we advocate for unapologetically. One need only envision an anti-domestic violence campaign that promotes "abuse-less Mondays" or "more humane abuse" to see how some methods of persuasion used for animal advocacy are not logical from a behavioral change or social justice standpoint.

No other behavioral change method (or social justice movement, for that matter) has suffered such a lack of a clearly identified end goal. If I were to suggest to my patients that a simple reduction of their violence towards women, or reliance on fewer abuse strategies, was acceptable and commendable as an end goal, I would be doing a great disservice to the victims and should lose my job. When I work with those who engage in violence, we work together to establish the goal of remaining non-violent. Again, if we want to see a specific behavior changed, ultimately end the violence, and help those affected, we need to be clear about *what* that behavior is and *why* it needs to change.

Reducing consumption of animal flesh and secretions is a step in the right direction so long that this reduction is part of an effort to go vegan. If we want to promote real change, we should be supporting these gains as much as we can, so long that we're careful not to convey the idea that any animal use is morally justifiable. These should be viewed as steps towards veganism rather than ends in and of themselves. So, to be clear, supporting others working to reduce consumption of animal products is not necessarily poor advocacy from a behavioral change perspective, as long as this reduction is part of a strategy with the objective of going vegan, not simply cutting back on animal use as an end goal.

This is where mainstream animal rights groups get it fundamentally wrong. We should never compromise the vegan message by suggesting that anything less than veganism is acceptable or ethical as an end goal. That does great harm to the movement and to those who are attempting to promote true veganism and the end of all animal use. There is never a need to weaken our message, since all of the science tells us that having clear long-term goals is the best way to facilitate motivation and help bring about behavioral change. Our goal should be to work on motivating people to go vegan; then, once they have made the commitment to do so, we can help them take the steps necessary to get there. That is a true behavioral change strategy.

Many individual animal advocates and organizations fear promoting veganism as an end goal because they feel that if they're too "pushy" they will lose people altogether. This is likely a leading factor in why a larger cultural shift towards veganism has not occurred. It is in fact possible—and optimal—to clearly state a goal of ending violence towards animals *and* work with non-vegans in a productive, non-aggressive manner to produce behavioral change.

Many of us (myself included) took many years to go vegan, and progressed from reducing animal consumption to transitioning to a plant-based diet and then veganism. Some argue that since they took a gradual approach, this is what we should be advocating for others. What they are missing, though, is that if they received clear vegan messaging to end all animal use, they may have gone vegan much sooner and prevented the deaths of many more animals. When we advocate for veganism as an end goal, people will naturally reduce their animal consumption, but will likely do so at a faster pace and will ultimately go vegan. Some will literally go vegan overnight.

Some animal advocates may also argue that it is simply more effective to ask people to cut down on animal use rather than asking them to go vegan. It is important to keep in mind that there is absolutely no scientific evidence for such claims, as I have discussed in Chapter 4, and this perspective is not based on any sound theoretical rationale for long-term behavioral change. In fact, such notions disregard a wealth of data showing that it is important to set clear long-term goals that involve a true discrepancy between that goal and current behavior.[5] In other words, it is counterproductive to "settle" for an easy-to-attain goal that the individual is likely to change without our intervention when we could be helping to set more challenging long-term goals to strive for, and that would represent truly internal behavioral change.

You might still be asking yourself, "That all sounds good, but what if the person I'm communicating with refuses to commit to going vegan?" My response is that I would expect the other person *not* to make that commitment when you first begin discussing veganism with them in particular. However, their resistance to committing to veganism does not mean that they are a lost cause by any means. Your communication with them may have helped stimulate some thoughts on the issue, and perhaps it will open the door to them having a follow-up discussion or conducting some research on their own. Few people go vegan after any one particular interaction, and we must not place too much pressure on ourselves to make others go vegan after any interaction. Making such a commitment is best thought of as a process, as I will be discussing more fully in Chapter 9. All that we can do is to help move them closer to choosing veganism, but we cannot force them to change, and we should not engage in desperate tactics such as asking them to reduce their animal use rather than promoting veganism because it is less conducive to long-term change.

We should also be mindful of our larger end goal at the societal level in our advocacy efforts. If our goal is to ultimately convince the world population that we must end all animal use, we should be treating veganism as an issue of social justice and should not encourage others to continue to think of animals as "products" for which we can continue to consume in moderation. We must be careful that our animal advocacy does not perpetuate oppressive views of nonhuman animals, which would ultimately be to their detriment.

CHAPTER 7

RELATIONSHIPS IN
VEGAN ADVOCACY

One thing I believe most animal rights groups have gotten right is highlighting the importance of the interpersonal relationship between the animal advocate and the non-vegan. Considerations of the "process" by which others undergo change, and finding ways to join with them, are critical for creating the conditions for positive change to occur. In fact, it has repeatedly been shown in the clinical psychology literature that the bond between the change agent and the change target is a stronger predictor of therapy outcome than the specific approach used.[1] In other words, the more we are able to join with those we are attempting to influence and develop a positive bond and sense of shared goals, the more influence we will have.

Some of my own research, including my doctoral dissertation, shows that the stronger the personal bond we develop with our violent clients, the more likely they are to end the violence and remain non-abusive.[2,3] While this may seem obvious to some of us, at the time I published this work there were many in the violence field who downplayed the importance of a positive therapeutic relationship in promoting change. Some believed that the processes of change that are relevant for every other problem behavior do not apply to those who use violence. My work in fact showed that developing a positive relationship may be the single most important factor in helping violent individuals end their violence.

It stands to reason that the same would be true for animal advocacy. If the person we're trying to reach feels connected to us and likes us, they are more likely to join with us in working on changing their behavior. There is a very important caveat to consider, however: Just liking the animal advocate is not enough, especially if the advocate is not clear in their advocacy. As mentioned earlier, if we're not clearly promoting veganism, then getting non-vegans to like us will not increase the chances that they will go vegan. I believe this is a major mistake made by many activists—they water down their vegan message so as not to upset others. While the non-vegan might appreciate not being challenged ethically, they will not be any more likely to actually stop contributing to the harm of animals.

When developing any behavioral change strategy, it's important to be genuine, straightforward, and clear about what it is that needs to change and why, without judging and making others defensive. Yes, this is possible and actually quite simple and therapeutic. One can show understanding and empathy for how a problematic behavior developed and what upholds that behavior while still maintaining a stance that all violence and exploitation must end. These concepts are not mutually exclusive, but are in fact necessary for lasting change to occur.

I have found that my patients appreciate my authenticity when I observe how specific behaviors are problematic. I also work to reinforce positive gains my patients make, even if they don't handle things perfectly. Of course when we reinforce positive behavior, this has a stronger impact than if we just focus on punishing the negative behavior. However, we never support or condone abusive behavior in any way, and we make a point to label abuse when it occurs.

We should be doing the same thing when it comes to our animal advocacy. Again, we should be clear in our end goals and reinforce positive gains, taking care to be kind and supportive within the context of working towards veganism. Just like in my interpersonal violence work, I have often discussed the ethics of animal use with non-vegans with terrific results. I have found that most non-vegans are receptive to a straightforward discussion about whether or not it is morally acceptable to use animals. This is a discussion that can happen in a respectful manner, remaining mindful that the non-vegan may be expecting us to attack them. When we can demonstrate the opposite—that veganism is really about justice for animals and living a kind life, and show that we have no interest in vilifying them—they will be much more likely to discuss their own interest in veganism.

Practice in "active listening" skills may be particularly helpful in relationship building efforts, as these skills form an integral component of the most effective relationship enhancement interventions.[4] When others feel that they have been listened to, it naturally follows that they will be more likely to listen to our perspective. One key aspect of active listening is to use paraphrasing, which involves reflecting back, in our own words, what the other person has said to demonstrate that we understand them. If we paraphrase accurately, the other person will likely feel more understood. If we are inaccurate with our paraphrase, this allows the other person to clarify the meaning of what they said. Active listening also involves asking open-ended questions to better understand the other's perspective, and validation to demonstrate that we can understand their perspective. For example, we can validate that it may be difficult for someone to cut out their consumption of dairy, and then discuss how we were able to do so ourselves.

When we use these active listening strategies, the non-vegan will typically become much less defensive and they will be more likely to listen to what we have to say, because we listened to and validated their perspective. These listening skills are key for enhancing any form of communication; every communication skills program begins with focusing on listening because these skills are by far most critical for seeing true change.

Even with the knowledge of how critical it is to improve our listening, these skills are almost always a great challenge to convey to others. I have given countless couples specific instructions about how to show their partner they are listening to the other, and then directly observed the couples doing the exact opposite of what I had asked them to do.

What gets in the way of teaching these skills? What makes it so hard for people to show that they are listening and understanding the other person? Many people are so focused on getting their point across that they completely ignore what the other person is saying. The focus becomes "winning" the discussion rather than having a true exchange of viewpoints. This notion of always having to win is ingrained in most of us from early in our lives and it carries over into our daily interactions. This becomes problematic in our relationships because it shuts down true communication. It also may lead to problems in our animal advocacy because the other person will not be interested in hearing our perspective if they feel that we haven't listened to theirs. We may in fact "win" the discussion about the ethics of eating animals and their secretions, but such a win is completely irrelevant if it doesn't bring the other person any closer to veganism.

How do we overcome these challenges to listening? The key to becoming a better listener is to focus on one's mindset. When we remind ourselves that our goal is to show the other person that we are listening to them and understanding their perspective, we will be much more effective in our communication. It is this change in mindset that will allow us to focus on having a true back and forth rather than a battle to show the other person that we are right and they are wrong.

Of course, just because we are listening to the other person and finding things to validate does not mean that we are agreeing with them. We can disagree with what they are saying completely but still show that we are listening and can understand where they are coming from. We can reflect back to them that we can see why they might feel that way, or perhaps we used to feel the same way, while at the same time explaining our own vegan perspective. I am not saying that we should be "wishy-washy" in our advocacy by any means. As I describe in the next chapter, being very clear and honest with our vegan advocacy is extremely important.

Similarly, we may perfectly demonstrate that we are listening to the non-vegan, and use textbook communication skills, and yet still not see any immediate change in the other person's perspective. This is to be expected. We cannot pin too much hope on bringing about change in a single interaction because behavioral change is much more complicated than that. However, through these conversations we may be planting seeds, or helping the non-vegan see things in a different way, which may move them closer to making actual behavioral changes than we realize. So it is important to not get too discouraged if we do not see an immediate impact on the part of the other person.

The adapted online discussion below illustrates the importance of relationship building and listening skills:

Jasmin: I'm a long-time vegetarian and want to be vegan. The problem is that I feel lonely and depressed a lot and the only time I really get out is when I go to my local diner that is not vegan. They do make me a vegetarian dish but they say they can't do vegan. I wish there was a vegan place to go to, but I live in a small town and there are no such places. We really need more vegan places in small towns like mine.

CT: Hi, Jasmin. That's awesome you want to go vegan! What a lot of vegans tell me is that they feel happier and healthier when they match their behavior with their love for animals. When you are doing what you can to reduce animal cruelty, you may notice changes in how you feel overall. That may mean finding a new place to eat or eating at home. Just keep in mind that your inconvenience pales in comparison to what these killed animals go through.

Jasmin: Trust me, I know this! I beat myself up all the time about the fact that I haven't gone vegan yet. I originally went vegetarian because I didn't want to hurt animals. The thing is, going out to this place is an important way that I'm able to battle my loneliness. I feel that I have to keep doing what I'm doing because this is how I'm able to take care of myself and keep myself from getting worse. I don't have any other good way of being around good people every day and getting support in person, so I think that means I can't go vegan right now.

CT: I understand that you feel like there is no good way to get the social interaction you need while going vegan at the same time. I know that sometimes it's scary to change routines, but you may find that you actually feel better if you did, especially since you are not happy now. It is possible that you will find that when you take that next step it will be just what you needed mentally or spiritually. When one knowingly lives in a manner that contradicts their basic ethics, it can be unhealthy and make things worse.

Jasmin: You're probably right that I will feel better if I rip off that Band-Aid and just do it. I have seen a lot of other vegans post online about how they feel a lot happier and healthier after going vegan. I just wish I had a solution to the diner issue because it's the one way I get any kind of face-to-face support.

CT: Even the greasiest diner should be able to give you a vegan meal. Do you have any other friends who you can spend time with?

Jasmin: I do have some good friends but none of them are vegan and they don't make vegan dishes when I go to their homes.

CT: That must be hard for you. Have you considered talking to the folks at the diner, and also to your friends, about how they can help support you by working with you to have vegan food? I'm guessing that if you told them that this was something important to you, they might be willing to help out.

Jasmin: That's a good idea. I think I will do that. I think at least my friends will understand. Maybe we can experiment together with vegan dishes and then I won't feel pressure to eat non-vegan food when I'm there. What I'd really like is to have real vegan friends someday. Thank you for listening to my situation, by the way. I appreciate you taking the time.

CT: I'm pretty confident that you will find other vegan friends to join you if you go vegan. It took me a while myself to find that. You might also want to check out local vegan groups and meet-ups, and look into joining online vegan groups.

Jasmin: Thank you. Okay, I'm going to give that all a try!

Notice in the above scenario that I worked to continuously listen to what Jasmin was saying and what she felt was getting in the way of her going vegan. I also validated her concerns and asked open-ended questions for her to tell me more about her situation. I did not accuse her of "making excuses" for remaining non-vegan, or criticize her for having difficulty in making the transition. She seemed to appreciate feeling listened to, and did not respond defensively when I suggested to her the benefits of matching her behavior with her care for animals. If I had approached this differently, by more aggressively challenging her at the outset, she likely would not have had as favorable a response and may have left this social media page never to return.

This interaction could potentially represent a turning point for Jasmin, or conversely, contribute to her feelings of loneliness and hopelessness regarding going vegan. Through supportive listening, and continuously emphasizing the value in going vegan, I was able to help her feel supported while at the same time encouraging her to make the transition to veganism that she really wanted to make.

CHAPTER 8

ASSERTIVE VEGAN COMMUNICATION

One of the key skills that any psychologist teaches their patients is assertiveness. In fact, if there were one skill that I could bestow upon every animal advocate, it would be assertiveness. The reason is that assertiveness is simply the best way to get one's point across and facilitate good communication.[1] Assertiveness also happens to be the best approach to get others to do what we want them to. So, if we want others to stop contributing to the exploitation of animals, assertive messaging is key.

To be assertive simply means to express oneself in a manner that is respectful of the other person, but also respectful of oneself. Being assertive means we are clearly letting others know how we feel, as well as setting limits for acceptable behavior. We are also respecting ourselves by expressing ourselves forthrightly, rather than keeping our feelings in. Assertiveness skills are key to increasing understanding and overcoming differences and conflict.

All too often, people communicate in overly passive or aggressive ways. We are essentially taught to be either passive or aggressive from childhood, and this message gets reinforced throughout our lives. To be passive means to stuff our feelings and avoid openly expressing them. The obvious problem with passivity is that not expressing one's feelings means that issues don't get resolved and can instead build up over time and lead to problems with aggression. To be aggressive means to attack others or otherwise confront them in a hostile manner. The problem with aggressive communication is that it puts others on the defensive, so they tune the aggressive person out or try to avoid them, assuming that the aggressive individual is irrational. Essentially, we lose credibility when we begin to attack the other person and our efforts are in vain because our message will be tuned out.

Many advocates keep their veganism and related beliefs about animal use to themselves out of fear of upsetting non-vegans by discussing ethics. This obviously does little to help the animals. While "living by example" does help show people the positive side of veganism, and can help affect true change, we can be even more effective as advocates by unapologetically speaking out for animals who cannot speak for themselves. If we want veganism and animal rights to be taken seriously as social justice issues, we can't be afraid to advocate for animals in a clear manner that calls for an end to all forms of exploitation.

Responding to non-vegans in an aggressive manner is also highly destructive, as it shuts down communication. When we communicate aggressively, others will not want to listen to what we have to say and we may lose a valuable chance to effectively advocate for animals. It can be difficult at times to control aggressive impulses, but we must remember that this is the best way to help animals. I can think of multiple occasions where I've felt I was reaching a non-vegan in my advocacy efforts, and those gains were quickly erased when another vegan advocate would offer their thoughts in a hostile or aggressive way.

When we're aggressive with non-vegans about their animal use, we often see that classic shame response I discussed earlier. Feelings of shame can prevent one from truly taking a personal inventory and thinking about how their behavior may be harming others. When one is shamed, they will be more likely to irrationally defend themselves and lash back out at the person who is aggressing towards them, which may further escalate the disagreement. This of course leads to a completely unproductive, or even counterproductive, interaction that makes a vegan transition far less likely.

Now, I want to be clear about what I mean by aggressive, because some people claim that those simply pointing out animal exploitation and injustice are being aggressive ("attacking") towards them. To be aggressive means to engage in name-calling, put-downs, yelling, or otherwise directly attacking the other person. The language we use can be aggressive, so we should be careful to use words that are most likely to get our vegan message across and least likely to induce shame in the other person or cause them to become defensive.

It is *not* aggressive, however, to let others know directly that their behavior is unethical, point out the harm others do to animals, or use logic and reason to point out poor arguments in defense of animal abuse. Ultimately, the key lies in how we express these things in our discussions with non-vegans. I have found that when a non-vegan feels they are "losing" a discussion about animal cruelty, they will sometimes claim that they're being "attacked" in an effort to exit the conversation and maintain their attitudes in support of animal exploitation. There is simply nothing that can be done about that. If others incorrectly accuse someone of being aggressive because they don't know what the term means, that's on them.

It seems that many vegans are terrified of representing the stereotype of vegans being "angry" in their dealings with non-vegans. The truth is that those who want vegans to stop advocating for animals are the ones who have propagated this stereotype. It's the same tactic that has been used in attempts to silence the voices of civil rights activists ("angry black people") and feminists ("angry man haters"). We as animal advocates should recognize that this is just a stereotype and not be silenced. To do so would be a great disservice to the movement and to the animals who needlessly suffer and die by the billions each year.

Communicating with non-vegans clearly and unapologetically about the ethics of animal use—in other words, assertively, while not attacking or disrespecting the other person (even if the other person is aggressive towards us) —is the best way to achieve productive communication and the possibility of a positive response to our message. I believe if all vegans and animal rights activists were assertive in their communication, we would see an enormous adoption of veganism and end a great deal of animal suffering. Assertiveness is a skill we can all work on, and it is sorely needed in the animal advocacy realm.

An important aspect of assertive animal advocacy is to know the facts about veganism. It's important that we convey to others that we are knowledgeable on the topic if we want them to listen to what we have to say. So we should have a good understanding of what animal agriculture involves and how animals are abused, and we should be familiar with the research on veganism and health, as well as the environmental impacts of animal agriculture. Perhaps most importantly, we should know how to respond to the common arguments we might hear from non-vegans, discussed in the following chapter.

Contrary to what many seem to believe, we can't turn someone off of veganism simply by discussing it assertively. I have never witnessed an occasion where someone was considering veganism and then completely reversed course when someone else attempted to engage them in a constructive manner.

Below are some examples of passive, aggressive, and assertive responses in the animal advocacy context:

Example #1
Andre: Veganism is just like another religion. Why don't you just live and let live and not bother those who don't subscribe to your extreme diet? I respect your views. Why can't you respect mine?

Passive Response: I agree with you. Your diet is your business. Some vegans are too pushy. Not all vegans though. Please don't judge us all because of some bad apples. (passive because doesn't advocate for animals when given the opportunity)

Aggressive Response: Why don't you go kill yourself? You murder animals and you expect me to respect that? Get lost. (aggressive because directly attacks the other person)

Assertive Response: Actually, veganism is not like a religion at all. Vegans are not asking you to believe something that we can't directly observe. It's a fact that billions of animals are killed every year for food and it's completely unnecessary. We can't respect the needless killing of animals. (assertive because it clearly presents the vegan view, advocating for animals, but does so in a non-attacking manner)

Example #2
Janice: I have a lot of respect for vegans. Good for you for showing such self-restraint. I could never do it, though. I love cheese too much!

Passive Response: Well, veganism isn't for everyone. (passive because doesn't advocate for animals when given the opportunity)

Aggressive Response: Did you know that mother cows are raped and baby cows are killed for your precious cheese? You are beyond selfish. (aggressive because engages in name calling)

Assertive Response: Of course you could do it! After you've been vegan for a month or so, you won't even miss animal foods. If you ever find yourself in a moment of weakness and need motivation, just think about the calves who are taken from their mothers at birth. (assertive because is supportive communication and makes point about animal cruelty without attacking the person)

Example #3

Robert: Veganism seems like a wonderful way to live and although I love meat I have had many great vegan dishes! However, the vegan lifestyle is really damn expensive and it feels exhausting for me to even consider getting started going vegan. Animal ingredients are in everything and it's just too much detective work and preparation for me.

Passive Response: Well, maybe this just isn't the right time for you to think about going vegan. It's a journey for most of us. (passive because doesn't directly address the issues raised and help Robert overcome his stated barriers)

Aggressive Response: So what it comes down to is that you're too lazy to stop killing animals. I guess you can't be bothered with having concern about other sentient beings. You really need to educate yourself. (aggressive because engages in name-calling)

Assertive Response: If you use a bunch of specialty products it can be expensive, but I personally spend way less as a vegan than I did when I was buying animal products. I buy a lot of rice, beans, pasta, fresh produce, etc. It saves me money at the grocery store and it'll save me money down the line in healthcare costs. I know it might feel daunting for you now, but I'm guessing you will find that it's a lot easier to go vegan than you think. (assertive because directly promotes veganism while not attacking the person)

CHAPTER 9

THE STAGES OF INTENTIONAL BEHAVIORAL CHANGE

The most common and egregious mistakes I have observed in animal advocacy involve how we respond to those who demonstrate at least some ambivalence about changing their behavior. I will provide two examples below of common mistakes that I witness regularly:

Steve: I'm a transitioning vegan. I have given up all meat and am working on dairy products. It's pretty easy after you see the horrific truth. I don't want to touch any kind of meat. I switched to certified humane eggs and milk and am having difficulty giving them up. I want to try out different alternative milks available. Also, it's hard for me to keep track of what to avoid in baked goods.

Response A / Passive Response
Robin: Steve, I know that some will disagree with what I'm saying, but make sure that you take your time to transition, and if you need to eat eggs, please try to cut down and make sure that you know where they're coming from and how the hens are treated. For many of us, going vegan was a journey and we need to be supportive.

Response B / Aggressive Response
Dominique: The baby chicks who are ground alive don't care about your vegan "journey." If you cared about animals you'd go vegan; it's as simple as that. When you buy so-called "humane" eggs, you're mur-

dering animals for the sake of your own taste buds.
It's time to get over yourself and focus on the animals.

This example illustrates what can happen when we hope to see immediate behavioral change when the non-vegan person demonstrates some ambivalence about changing. In both cases, the animal advocate is attempting to promote some immediate behavior change, but using different approaches and emphasizing different end goals. For "Response A," Robin is making the mistake of passively "settling" for an end goal less than veganism in the hopes of seeing some immediate change, consistent with the reducetarian approach. For "Response B," Dominique is more aggressively challenging Steve in an effort to "jolt" him into going vegan immediately. Neither response is likely to be effective because neither of them will likely serve to move the individual any closer to veganism.

It is critically important to keep in mind that our ability to influence the behavior of others is not determined by how that individual responds immediately in the moment. Indeed, it's fairly rare to make such a compelling point that the non-vegan will voice their decision to go vegan right then and there. What is most important is that we help that individual to increase their own readiness for changing their behavior and going vegan. For some, our discussion with them may "tip the balance" in favor of changing and they may go vegan shortly after. For others, our interaction with them may not get them to go vegan immediately, but it may help them think more about the ethical implications of their animal use, setting the stage for both short-term and long-term behavioral change.

A maddening statement that both vegans and non-vegans often make is: "The world isn't going to go vegan overnight." This phrase is used to justify advocating the "baby steps" approach where we don't encourage people to go vegan, which often leads to people stopping short of veganism altogether because they think they're doing enough by eating less meat or switching to almond milk. The reason this argument doesn't hold water is because it ignores the fact that behavioral change occurs at the individual level, and many people literally do go vegan overnight! Therefore, the baby steps theory is no justification for advocating anything less than veganism.

Just because it may have taken us many years to go fully vegan doesn't mean we wouldn't have made the change much sooner if others had more openly discussed veganism with us. I personally went vegan when a friend of mine assertively confronted me about my vegetarianism and how I was contributing to the harm done to animals in the dairy industry. I knew she was right, and I went vegan that day. I have heard many stories similar to mine from other long-time vegans.

The change process, however, is certainly different for different people, and it is important for us to match our strategy for promoting change to the stage where the individual is in terms of their readiness for change. This is critical in our attempt to help anyone change a problematic behavior that they may not recognize as problematic. Again, however, the explicit end goal of veganism should not change regardless of our strategy.

An influential theoretical model, originally developed in the treatment of alcoholics and adapted for a range of other problematic behaviors, is the Transtheoretical Model, or stages of change model.[1] In its simplest form, the model states that when we change a problematic behavior, we go through a series of stages ranging from a phase where we are not even considering changing to a phase where we have fully changed the behavior. This model has also led to specific "Motivational Interviewing" techniques that have shown to effectively promote therapeutic change across a number of treatment populations.[2,3]

To briefly summarize the model, the specific stages of change are:

Stage 1 — Pre-contemplation: The individual does not recognize that their behavior needs changing. In the context of animal advocacy, the individual may proudly consume animal "products" and state that they have no intention of ever changing.

Stage 2 — Contemplation: The person first begins to consider the merits of changing the behavior. They may ask for information about vegan nutrition or recipes, or ask about videos that show the cruelty of the animal agriculture industry.

Stage 3 — Preparation: The individual perceives a need to change and is getting ready to do so. They may indicate that it's time for them to go vegan and that they are ready to take that final step.

Stage 4 — Action: The individual is actively working on changing the behavior. Here, the individual is in the early stages of their transition to veganism and is changing their routines.

Stage 5 — Maintenance: The behavioral change has been made and the individual is working to prevent relapsing to their old ways. This phase is critical because a relapse is a very real concern, though the more one resonates with ethical arguments of veganism related to minimizing our harm to animals, the less likely they are to revert to non-veganism.

An important aspect of this model is that when a person experiences a relapse, they don't necessarily go back to the pre-contemplation stage of change. After a relapse one can return to any of the previous stages, and it should be our goal as advocates to get them back to the action and maintenance stages. This model is very important in helping us think about what an individual may need as they transition through the different stages of the change process.

Pre-Contemplation Stage Tips

If changing is not even on a person's radar (pre-contemplation), consciousness-raising messages have been shown to help people recognize the ethical consequences of their current path. If they're content consuming animal products, simply leading by example and telling them about the wonders of vegan food will have little or no impact.

The pre-contemplation stage is where you will find many of the common justifications for using animals:

- What about plants? Plants have feelings too!
- We have been eating animals since the beginning of time. It is responsible for our brain growth and we have developed canines to eat animals.
- The bible says that we should eat animals.
- Animals eat other animals. Would you ask a lion to go vegan?
- We are part of the food chain. It's the way it is. Things must die for us to live.
- If we didn't breed cows to eat, they would not exist, so isn't it better they have a chance to live?
- I always give thanks when I eat meat and we try to use the whole animal.
- There are essential vitamins in meat that we can't get from just eating vegetables.
- They are just animals. What's the difference if we eat them? They don't care whether they live or die anyways.
- If the world went vegan, animals would overrun the planet.

- Vegans are hypocrites. I know a vegan who wears leather and feeds his cats other animals.
- Not everyone can be vegan. What about the Inuit?

There are many, many more of these justifications you will have heard if you are a long-time vegan. Other sources provide a more complete list with possible responses you could offer when you encounter them.[4,5]

When encountering justifications for using animals such as these, it's important not to get sucked into an argument. It's always best to maintain your composure and provide factual and ethical responses. If it becomes clear that the other person really has no interest in learning more about veganism, but rather wants to continue to justify animal abuse or prove you wrong, it's usually best to let them know that there's really no point in discussing further and you're always happy to discuss these issues at another time. What sometimes happens in discussions with those in the pre-contemplation stage is that because they're not ready to hear a vegan message, they may attempt to bait you into an argument, and then when you lose your composure, they will accuse you of being just another "crazy vegan." So don't take the bait; instead just focus on demonstrating that these are topics you've researched and thought a lot about.

The more you come across like someone who has a command of this information, the more expert you will appear, and the more likely the other person will listen to what you have to say. The same is true in clinical psychology more broadly; it's critically important that our clients believe that we know what we're talking about and we have the knowledge and ability to help them achieve their desired end goals.

I have personally observed some move from the pre-contemplation stage all the way to going vegan, so even when our advocacy efforts may seem hopeless with these individuals, keep in mind that change is still possible. They may not go vegan right away, but it can certainly happen. However, for many in the pre-contemplation stage, battling it out with them can be draining and may not always be the best use of our time as advocates, since there are so many pre-vegans who are further along in their readiness for change and just need help in getting that final push to make the transition.

Contemplation Stage Tips

If the individual is considering going vegan (contemplation), we can work with them in an attempt to tip the balance towards living a life consistent with their values of justice and compassion for others. The ethical case for veganism is very important for those in the contemplation stage (as well as the other stages) because ethics is our strongest, most compelling argument. Those in the contemplation stage are open to hearing about how the needless killing of animals is incompatible with their views of social justice and kindness towards others. This openness enables the person to see past how we have been socially conditioned to accept animal exploitation and instead consider the impacts of their non-vegan-ism on others.

An important tenet of the stages of change model and moti-vational interviewing techniques designed to increase readiness for change is the idea that speech *is* behavior. By that I mean that if we can encourage the other individual to make statements in favor of changing, this is actual change-relevant behavior because actions follow our intentions.[6] The entire basis of motivational interviewing is to elicit change-relevant verbalizations because we tend to align our behavior with our intentions and our thoughts about changing.

For this reason, I find that one of the most important questions I ask non-vegans, particularly those in the contemplation stage, is "Are you interested in going vegan?" What I have found is that when non-vegans are in the contemplation stage of change, they often will immediately respond "yes" to this question and they exhibit a sense of relief about making this public commitment. If they are truly in the contemplation stage, even if they don't affirmatively respond to this question, they will let me know what the remaining barriers might be, which allows for a useful conversation about how to overcome these barriers.

The animal advocate's assessment of the other's readiness for change is important in deciding the best way to approach them. If the advocate can correctly diagnose the situation and determine where the non-vegan individual is in terms of their readiness for change, they will then be positioned to use an effective strategy that matches their stage of change. A simple question like "Are you interested in going vegan?" may in fact be the most powerful intervention that can be provided to the non-vegan depending on their current mindset and readiness level.

Below is a portion of an adapted discussion I have had on the Vegan Publishers Facebook page that highlights a non-vegan who is in the contemplation stage, and how I responded to him:

> *Andy*: People want to ignore what happens to these animals. I'm not vegan but I do see what is going on. We're pumping hormones into these animals that we are killing and eating. I've read books and watched videos about how these animals are tortured. It stresses them out. There's no way that can be healthy. But there are organic options that I do agree with. But everyone's entitled to their own opinion. As much as I would love to quit eating meat, it's a difficult habit to give up.
>
> *CT*: It sounds like you agree with veganism, so how can we help you go vegan? If you've read up on it I'm sure you know that "organic meat" is also cruel to animals.
>
> *Andy*: True, I just need to find a good place to start.

CT: We can definitely help you with that. What information would be most helpful for you to go vegan?

The reason I would categorize this person in the contemplation stage is because she expressed concern about animals while also displaying ambivalence about changing. In instances like this, a motivational approach would be to side with her reasons for changing and to lead her towards making more statements in favor of going vegan. Attempting to focus on the ambivalence in this instance would likely be counterproductive and she would likely respond defensively, becoming more entrenched in her ambivalence.

Notice here that I could have easily just said "good for you" for only eating "organic" or humane meat, and urged her to simply cut down on animal consumption rather than go vegan. If I had done that, I would have missed a valuable opportunity to move someone closer to veganism, reducing collective demand for animal "products" and ultimately preventing the needless killing of thousands of animals over the course of her lifetime. What we need to keep in mind here is that while she may not decide to go vegan right on the spot, she's now clearly considering veganism and is surely on a vegan path. My next focus is then to support her in giving her the information and resources she needs as she moves into the preparation and action stages of change.

Preparation Stage Tips

When somebody demonstrates readiness to go vegan (preparation), all they may need are the information, skills, and tools to do so. In this case, helping them make the transition with tips for living a life with less cruelty and exposing them to examples of happy, healthy vegans can be particularly helpful. Helping them shop, providing recipes, and suggesting products free of animal ingredients or testing are very important ways to help them avoid feeling overwhelmed by the upcoming transition.

It is also critically important to be encouraging and hopeful for their prospects for changing. Letting them know that we believe that they can do it and that we were in their shoes at one time can be a big help. Perhaps they have made other substantial life changes and we can point out that they were successful in making those other changes, so going vegan should be something they can do as well.

Here's an example of an (adapted) email that I received from someone in the preparation stage, and my response. I receive these kinds of emails on a daily basis:

> **Betty**: Hi, I'm currently breastfeeding and I really want to become vegan. Can you please lead me towards some sources, or tell me what kinds of foods I need to be eating while on the vegan diet? I am also trying to lose weight.

> **CT**: Hi Betty, that's awesome and congrats on the baby! We had a beautiful vegan baby ourselves and she's healthy and happy. The best book to absolutely get is Everything Vegan Pregnancy.[7] That book will have all the info you need.

> **Betty**: Thanks! I will get that book!

These interactions may seem small and insignificant, but this kind of supportive communication can make a huge difference for those transitioning to veganism. Anything we can do to be supportive and to help the person get to the point where they've overcome any barriers to making the vegan transition can be of enormous value.

Action and Maintenance Stage Tips

Perhaps the best thing we can offer those in the action and maintenance stages is our support and encouragement. Recognizing that the person is working hard to change their previous long-standing behavior patterns regarding animal use, and re-assuring them that it will get easier, can be very helpful during this time. It is also important to encourage them to become a part of the vegan community, whether in their local area or online, if they are to maintain their success long-term. Sometimes vegans simply need to vent to other vegans and need a "safe space" where others understand their experiences in order to feel supported and maintain their conviction. The more we empower vegans, the more likely they are to engage in advocacy efforts to spread the vegan message themselves.

Here's an example of an (adapted) email I received from someone in the maintenance stage, along with my response:

Amanda: Hi! I am vegan now but had a thought this morning. Does eating meat from animals fed carcinogens etc. or that have cancer increase cancer risks in humans? Is there an increased risk of cancer among those who eat meat? There's a lot of cancer in my family history and I'm concerned for my parents.

CT: Hi Amanda, thanks for reaching out, and good for you for going vegan! Yes, eating animals increases cancer risk. There is a fair amount of research on the topic now and the World Health Organization has recently announced something to this effect. There are some great pages you might want to follow, such as the Physicians Committee for Responsible Medicine and A Guide to Vegan Nutrition.

In this example, I tried to be supportive and encouraging, and provided information that I thought would be helpful and that would also keep her on the vegan path. I also provided resources to keep her tuned into the vegan community.

Matching Our Approach with Stage of Change

As we become more skilled as animal advocates and behavioral change agents, we will find it easier to recognize in which stage the individual can be categorized, and can then deploy the most appropriate intervention to help them move through the stages of change. It would be just as pointless, for example, to give vegan nutritional advice to someone not even considering going vegan as it would to provide basic vegan education to someone who has already gone vegan and intends to stay that way.

These considerations of the stages of change model highlight that it is absurd when some advocates claim that a singular strategy should be used for everyone. Of course, people are more complicated than that, and what motivates one person to change may not work for another. Different people require different messages. Proven behavioral change efforts have been built around the idea that we need to meet people where they are in terms of changing and find the best method to tip the balance in favor of behavioral change for individuals who differ in beliefs and level of motivation.

We need to end the mindset that we know the singular, successful message for everyone. As with most things, we need multiple messages that target the issue from various directions so we will have a greater likelihood of success in promoting veganism. We still have much to learn about what works in different situations and with different individuals. Learning to engage in effective messaging is a process for all of us; one that does not simply consist of experts disseminating a body of codified facts.

As behavioral change agents, we need to recognize that we can only do so much to move someone along the stages of change. We as animal advocates all encounter individuals who are at the pre-contemplation stage, and little that we tell them can make them care about animals. There will be times when we will have done and said all that we possibly could, and will have to let it go. We can't make others change when they actively refuse to do so and are not open to a more compassionate message. This can be very frustrating to activists, especially when those we're trying to influence are our own loved ones.

All we can do is provide information and education whenever possible and hope that they will become more receptive to the message. Never forget that there are many people out there who will be receptive to the vegan message. So don't let a negative response prevent you from advocating for animals another day with a new audience.

Below is an example of a Facebook discussion (adapted) for which the issue of matching our approach to the individual's stage of change is highly relevant:

John: What would we do with cows and chickens if we didn't eat them? What purpose do they serve other than food? Wouldn't they go extinct? I know we don't HAVE to eat them, but we can and I prefer to eat meat than tofu for my protein.

Carol: What purpose do you or anyone else serve to the world? How important do you think you are? What level of contribution do we require from someone to avoid being killed? You come across as extremely ignorant.

Steve: Spoken like a true carnist. Cows and chickens and other animals are sentient beings just like cats and dogs. I assume you eat cats too, right?

John: Sorry that I made you guys mad. I was asking as a legitimate question, not to be a jerk or anything.

Steve: Well you are on a vegan site so how did you expect people would respond to your saying that animals serve no purpose other than to feed selfish humans? You won't find anyone here telling you that you're lovely for such comments and that you should go eat some bacon. Either you're here because you want to learn more about veganism or you're here to provoke others. I hope it's the former if you have compassion in your heart, but if not, then why are you here?

John: I feel a lot of compassion for animals, really. I'm studying to be a clinical psychologist now so that I can help others. I don't understand why people should be attacked over their nutritional choices though. This post showed up on my newsfeed because a friend "liked" it. I posed this question in the hopes of getting a serious answer because it's something I've been thinking about lately. I was hoping to get real answers, not hatred from vegans. I wasn't trying to be rude or upset anyone.

Carol: Your comment was snarky, ignorant, rude, and hypocritical, and now you're trying to play innocent. I have no tolerance for ignorance when it comes to animal abuse. You're the one eating animal corpse so you're the aggressive one here. You're not learning much in school.

John: Carol, I didn't post my question to be attacked by you. I'm just asking honest questions and all that you're telling me is that you're a rude human being.

Barbara: Hi John, veganism is at its core about preventing harm to sentient animals. It's a social justice movement. Vegans believe that nonhuman animals have the right to exist on their own terms. The dietary aspect of veganism is only incidental.

John: Thanks Barbara, that's helpful. Just so I understand, and I'm not trying to be rude, but is the reason people go vegan so that they don't feel bad about harming sentient animals? Please let me know if I have that right. I'm just trying to understand the reasoning.

Steve: Nobody is turning on you here. Just because we don't give you the answer you want you accuse us of attacking you. You should know that your questions would provoke us. We get this kind of crap all the time. If you care more about your appetite than the lives of others, then knock yourself out. Did you seriously think there was nothing wrong with what you were saying?

Carol: Do you think it's okay to eat other people with less intelligence, like babies and the mentally retarded? How do you prove the intelligence of animals or lack thereof? You're completely ignorant if you're using humans as your benchmark. Do you judge fish as less intelligent than humans because they can't do the same things as us? Are humans less intelligent because they're not able to do what other animals can do?

Steve: The problem with your mindset is that you seem to think that all animals are here for humans to use. I personally see all animals as equals on this planet.

John: Carol, please stop assuming things about me. Your attacks are baseless and I implore you to stop attacking me.

CT: John, I suggest that you check out the movie *Earthlings* on Netflix. The film is really helpful for those who are first trying to learn about animal agriculture and the reasons why vegans feel we should not be using animals for any purpose.

John: Thanks, I will definitely watch that as soon as my finals are over. I will give it a shot.

CT: Sounds great. Thanks for keeping an open mind and feel free to ask more questions. Good luck with your finals.

Carol: John, I'm sorry that you think I'm attacking you for challenging your ridiculous carnist comments. Yes, I'm challenging your garbage ideas and won't stop questioning your nonsense.

CT: Carol, I think John is at the very beginning of learning about this. I think he's earnest in his lack of knowledge about veganism. Let's take him at his word and have him watch *Earthlings* and see if he comes back with a new perspective. I think this was productive.

John: My question was about why we should be vegan when we have the options to eat animals for nutrition. I heard that the answer is because animals "have a right to exist on their own terms," though I'm not sure that I agree. You did question my education and my existential reason for living, which I take as a personal offense. I was raised in a family of cattle farmers, so I have not had reliable, unbiased information on the subject, and that's why I was here asking these questions. I appreciate those who are trying to give helpful comments, but your comments are neither informative nor helpful.

Carol: No, you asked what benefit there was to not killing and eating animals, which is pure ignorance. Then you asked how these animals were contributing to the world, which is also pure ignorance. Then you said they're not going extinct to try to justify killing them. Again, that's pure ignorance. Then you said we don't have to eat them but you prefer them for your protein as a final attempt to justify killing and eating animals. If you're going to be a therapist, you need to do some soul searching first.

John: Carol, I see that all you want to do is degrade my thoughts and comments because you don't agree with them. I understand that you feel compassion for animals but it doesn't give you a right to bombard me like you've done here. As far as I'm concerned, my conversation with you is done here. Others have given me adequate answers and further sources for helping my understanding. Continue to comment all you want, but know that they will accomplish nothing other than make me question the culture of this group.

This discussion is a good example of a failure to accurately diagnose the stage of change of the individual and to match our strategy with their level of motivation. John was clearly in the contemplation stage of change. He appeared to be at the very beginning of his questioning of our use of nonhuman animals and posed some questions to the group that may have come across as naïve to some and intentionally provocative to others. The most helpful approach at this stage would be to give John accurate information about veganism and to assist him in his thinking about our use of animals. It would also be more productive to assume that he has honest intentions of learning more rather than assuming that he is simply trying to upset those who care deeply about animals. A more aggressive, attacking approach to someone in the contemplation stage of change will only increase resistance and move someone further away from the goal of ultimately ending their use of animals.

This discussion also illustrates the importance of understanding when to end a discussion, recognizing that we have done all that we can do to help move someone to the next stage of change without pushing too hard. To have John agree to watch *Earthlings* (often referred to as "the vegan maker") is a big win for this discussion, and we should be happy to conclude the conversation with this on his "to do" list. Continuing the conversation by challenging his original question and motives further is not going to be helpful for the animals or anyone else for that matter. As vegan advocates we need to recognize when we have done all that we can do and move on.

Thinking of Non-Vegans as Pre-Vegans

It logically follows from the stages of change model that many of those who are not currently vegan will be vegan someday, just like most vegans were non-vegan at one point. This may be helpful for the animal advocate to always keep in mind. We cannot expect everyone to truly recognize the devastating harm we do to nonhuman animals at the same time that we do. It can be helpful to think of non-vegans the same way that we think of ourselves before we went vegan. Even the most offensive non-vegan who is in the pre-contemplation stage of change has the potential to someday go vegan. I have heard many vegans tell me that they once used to "troll" vegan Facebook pages, making hateful comments about loving the taste of animals, and yet they ended up going vegan.

If we want to have an assertive, thoughtful response to non-vegans who challenge us about our veganism, we will be most successful if we try to have an understanding of the place they're coming from—their current stage of change—and to recognize that this stage is not fixed. Just like us, they too will hopefully recognize the harm they do to animals and will take steps to eliminate it. This more hopeful perspective can help us to continue to advocate for animals regardless of how much resistance we receive, because we know that our efforts will ultimately pay off even if we don't see the immediate change we hope for.

A Simple Exercise: Pros and Cons of Behavioral Change

In my clinical work with violent individuals, one of the most productive motivational interviewing exercises I use to facilitate greater motivation and to tip the balance in favor of change is a simple "pros and cons" exercise.[8] This is exactly what it sounds like; I ask them what are the pros of changing versus not changing, writing them down so that we can review both categories afterwards. This way we can see if their current behavior is really working for them or not, and can envision what making the change might look like as they apply it to their lives.

In the context of helping others go vegan, we would simply ask the non-vegan what the benefits would be if they were to go vegan. Some possible responses we might anticipate are: feeling better about themselves for not harming animals, feeling like they have brought their behavior in line with their values, improving health, losing weight, and helping with the climate change problem and other environmental destruction. Possible "cons" of going vegan might be: difficulties with non-vegan loved ones who don't understand, difficulties around holidays, not being sure what to eat, concerns about how to get good vegan nutrition, and apprehension that vegan food will not taste as good.

Once these pros and cons are all written down in different columns, we can assist the person in reviewing them. It is especially useful to highlight the pros of changing and then doing some "reality testing" with the cons. For example, we can discuss how a vegan diet is extremely healthy if done right, or how our taste buds shift when we go vegan and we don't miss eating animals or their secretions at all.

The aim of this exercise, as with the goals for all of our communication attempts to promote vegan advocacy, should be to have an open discussion about the benefits of veganism and what gets in the way for them to go vegan. The more we can demonstrate that the pros of going vegan are numerous and far outweigh the cons, the more likely it is that the non-vegan will demonstrate a willingness to go vegan.

CHAPTER 10

ADVOCACY COMMUNICATION TRAPS

Beyond some of the pitfalls I've discussed, such as failure to consider the stages of change or engaging in overly passive or aggressive advocacy, there are a number of other traps that advocates can fall into that I think are counterproductive to helping animals.

Focusing on the Negative

When we're communicating with someone about nonhuman animals and are hoping to see change in their behavior, it is helpful to focus on the positive of what they're saying and doing. It's not always easy, but a fundamental law of human behavior is that we promote greater change when we reinforce positive behavior than when we punish negative behavior. Sometimes it means searching for that small kernel of positivity, such as voicing care for animals, and then highlighting and emphasizing that in our response.

What often happens is that when we hear certain myths about veganism or animals in general, our tendency is to launch right into our rebuttals and attempt to counter such misconceptions, and some may be inclined to go into attack mode. If there is something positive for us to reflect back to the other person, then we can better join with them in deciding that it's time to make a change. Here's a recent adapted example from the Vegan Publishers Facebook page:

Mandy: Honestly, I don't think animals really care about whether they live or die. They are not humans. Sorry.

CT: Mandy, in all honesty, do you think that this cow wanted to live? [sends link to a non-graphic video of a cow who shows intense fear before being slaughtered]

Mandy: I have lived around farms my whole life and I see a lot of happy cows who live pretty good lives. Maybe things are different where I am.

Mandy: Ugh, I just watched the video you sent. That's really horrible. What a scared little guy.

Mary: You are really a flaming idiot if you think that animals don't care whether they live or die! A true moron! These animals scream in terror at slaughterhouses and beg for their lives. Your ignorance is unreal! You need to go to a slaughterhouse yourself.

Mandy: This is exactly the reason why I don't want anything to do with the vegan world. So many vegans are hateful, nasty people who just look for things to criticize in others. You should be ashamed of yourselves! Every time I express an opinion in this group I am attacked by someone calling me a terrible person. I am in this group because even though I grew up with eating meat as being normal, there are some things that I really don't agree with, and I wanted to learn more and see the vegan perspective. I don't get how people can be against cruelty to animals but then are so mean to other humans! I have been researching veganism for the past couple of days, reading about it and watching any video I can find. I'm not against the idea of going vegan myself but I will never go vegan if it means that I will turn into a nasty person myself.

CT: Let's keep the focus on that cow in the video rather than someone here who offended you, because veganism is about the animals, not us. I understand why you feel attacked, and I don't condone it myself, but whether you go vegan or not should not depend on somebody else. It should only be about whether you make the decision minimize harm done to other animals. I'm really glad that you're looking into veganism and that you're keeping an open mind. I hope that you continue to come to this group and offer your thoughts, and ask for any help you need in going vegan. Also feel free to email me directly for any guidance I can offer.

Mandy: Thanks. I'm definitely willing to keep talking about it and I will take you up on your offer. That kind of stuff just puts me off.

In the above example, Mandy clearly displayed ambivalence about going vegan by voicing the myth that animals don't care whether they live or die. It can be frustrating for activists—who care deeply about animals and know them to be thinking, feeling beings—to hear someone voice such absurd rationalizations for killing animals. However, if we want to help animals, in cases such as this, we should be seeking for something positive to reinforce rather than aggressively attacking the negative comments.

In this example, after I was able to provide some corrective information to Mandy about animal sentience via a video link, Mandy indicated that she was affected by it, providing a small window to help move her along the stages of change. This productive conversation was thwarted, however, when Mary jumped in aggressively. I was forced to reenter the conversation and attempt to have Mandy refocus on the animals, and I praised her for researching veganism and keeping an open mind, and she seemed to respond favorably. The last thing that I'd want from this interaction would be for her to decide to unfollow our page and move further away from veganism.

The same general approach also holds when we hear someone explain how they've tried to go vegan but was not successful in some way. Our best approach here is to always ask them if they're ready to give it another try, or to have a discussion about what gets in the way of them going vegan:

> *Jay*: The day I tried to be vegan was the day I craved a cheeseburger. I almost never want a cheeseburger. SMH!

> *CT*: If you could go back and do it again, what would you do differently?

> *Jay*: I would remind myself why I wanted to go vegan in the first place. I will think about that *Earthlings* video that I watched.

> *CT*: Excellent! Sounds like you're disappointed in yourself, but you're resolved to not let that happen again. Are you ready to try to go vegan again?

> *Jay*: Yes I am! I just need to find a way to be stronger in those moments and remember the animals.

> *CT*: Good plan! Sounds great! You're going to do it. I have no doubt!

Here again, I could have focused on this person's failure to go vegan and told them they were selfish for giving in to their own desires rather than considering the life of the animal that they ate, but that would have been completely counterproductive to the goal of helping them go vegan. Instead, my focus was on helping them learn from this failure experience and getting them right back into the action stage of change. The more that we can encourage others to openly state that their plan is to go vegan, the more likely it is that they will in fact go vegan, so this interaction could be an important step in helping Jay truly make the commitment that is needed to make that permanent transition.

Allowing the Conversation to Get Sidetracked

Oftentimes when we attempt to have a discussion about our use of animals, the conversation can spiral into several different directions. We should see this for what it often is: the other person we're speaking with may wish to avoid a direct discussion of the ethics of our animal use. Therefore, the discussion may go in all kinds of unproductive directions, such as what cavemen ate, canine teeth, what animals in the wild eat, and whether or not plants can feel pain too. When this happens, it's usually best to refocus the conversation back to the ethical issue because that is our strongest and most defensible argument.

Astra: This vegan stuff is all just stupid mumbo-jumbo. Meat is food for humans and has been since the beginning of time. We're designed to eat meat; that's why we have these canines. You won't go to the jungle and lecture to a cheetah not to eat those antelopes anymore, would you?

CT: Unlike cheetahs, humans have no biological need to eat other animals. It's not even healthy for us. Since it's unnecessary, it's not ethical. What humans ate a long time ago has no bearing on our current food choices. What matters is whether it's defensible to eat animals right now, in the current time, given the immense suffering it causes to animals and the destruction it does to the planet. There is no question that we have no need to kill and eat animals or their secretions, so it can't be ethical to continue to do so.

In conversations such as this, with an individual who is in the pre-contemplation stage of change, it will do us no good to debate about our prehistoric diets or whether we're "designed" to eat animals or not. The most important point that we want to continue to bring back to the discussion is that it can't be ethical to continue to eat animals and their secretions when we have no need to do so whatsoever. This is an irrefutable fact that is at the heart of our vegan argument.

Mindreading

Mindreading is something that we all do, but it can be a hindrance to positive communication. When we assume we know what others are thinking and feeling, we are often wrong, and typically we are more likely to bias things in the negative direction rather than the positive direction. So it's helpful to try to never assume that we know what the other person is thinking, and instead, ask them directly. If we ever are unsure of something and engage in any form of mindreading, it's always best to assume the best rather than the worst.

> **_Example:_** *David's partner, Fiona, arrived a half hour late for a romantic dinner at a vegan restaurant. David has been talking to Fiona about why his veganism is important to him and he'd really like her to join him in going vegan. He's been planning this dinner for weeks, wanting to show her what great vegan food tastes like.*
>
> **_David_**: Obviously you showed up late because you resent me for being vegan and for trying to talk to you

about it. Next time just be more up front and tell me that you're not interested.

Fiona: What? No, my father fell down in the shower today so I had to rush over to check on him. He was okay but I was really stressed out and I guess I forgot to call you to let you know. I was really looking forward to dinner with you tonight, but if you're too mad now, we can do this another time.

In this example, David miscommunicated with Fiona because he made a negative assumption about her intentions, potentially ruining the nice evening he had planned. He would have been much better off simply asking Fiona about why she was late rather than assuming that it had something negative to do with her views on veganism.

CHAPTER 11

TARGETING CORE THEMES

There has been increasing recognition of intersections between different forms of oppression that include animal use.[1, 2] Intersectionality is the study of overlapping social identities and recognition of systems of oppression that are connected and share common root causes.[3, 4] The concept of intersectionality, as originally presented by legal scholar Kimberle Crenshaw, focused on recognizing the intersections between race and gender oppression, though Crenshaw later explained how it applied to various forms of identity,[5] and the model has since been expanded by activists to connect human and nonhuman oppression.[6]

From a psychological perspective, the search for root causes, or core themes, for problematic behaviors is of central importance, and if we can get at the underlying issues for multiple problems, we are doing the most important work that can be done. For example, across a range of therapy types and theoretical orientations, while we teach our clients specific techniques to develop particular skills, the mechanism of change for such clinical work is accessing the underlying issues that account for the entire range of problematic thoughts, feelings, and behaviors. Thus, we are better able to bring about change when we can access the core issues that underlie the difficulties. This has been shown to be particularly true when we are attempting to influence those engaging in behaviors that are especially difficult to change.[7]

The same can be said for issues of social justice. At the root of speciesism, racism, sexism, ableism, ageism, homo- and trans-antagonism, and other "isms" is the notion that some individuals are "lesser" than others. If we can get people to recognize that none of us are any "higher," "better," or "more deserving" than any other, we can bring about great change. This means that, as activists, we should not just be countering injustice towards nonhuman animals, but injustice in all its forms. We can all be much more effective as activists if we stand against oppression and build allies across these various issues.

As someone who has worked his entire career fighting for an end to domestic violence, I have at times found it staggering how cut off most my colleagues are from issues of animal exploitation and abuse. Every year I spend a weekend at a think tank where some of the greatest minds in the field of interpersonal violence gather to try to bridge gaps across advocacy efforts focusing on violence towards women, child abuse, elder abuse, community violence, etc., and come up with effective violence reduction campaigns and strategies. Vegan food is very hard to come by at these events, so literally hundreds of animals needlessly died to feed these humans who are supposed to be finding ways to end needless violence.

On the other hand, I have often witnessed vegans dismissing humans who experience oppression. They may say that they need to speak up for nonhuman animals only, and not humans who experience injustice, because nonhuman animals "don't have a voice," dismissing the fact that humans are also often voiceless against the oppression they experience. This stance not only reinforces the notion that vegans don't care about people, but also alienates potential allies from the vegan community.

Creating "safe spaces" has long been considered critical in clinical psychology, particularly with trauma-informed approaches that recognize the need to show understanding and sensitivity to others so that they will feel comfortable in truly joining with us.[8] We need to create safe spaces for animal advocacy that are free of oppressive speech or behavior, or else we risk re-victimizing already oppressed individuals whom we should be bringing into the movement, not repelling. There is no place for any form of oppressive or hateful speech in the animal advocacy community. Unfortunately, creating safe spaces and understanding the importance of bringing others into the movement are not high priorities for many mainstream animal advocacy groups, which hinders our ability to grow as a social justice movement.

Part of creating that safe space is being thoughtful about how we use comparisons that may be considered offensive by some, such as those involving human slavery. It is not advisable to directly compare the severity or magnitude of different forms of injustice or make judgments about whether one injustice is equal to or worse than another. There is no value in doing so, and it leads to a high potential for conflict with those whom we are attempting to reach. However, we should be able to discuss similarities in underlying systems of oppression or factors allowing for the injustice to occur.[9] Using language that is sensitive to linked oppressions is not "thought policing" or "political correctness." It promotes justice for all and invites other activists into the animal advocacy movement.

Despite potential barriers for other marginalized groups to join the vegan movement, people of color are about twice as likely to be vegan as white people.[10] Our movement directly benefits from continuing to value and amplify these voices to encourage a truly diverse, unified community that reflects our population, rather than presenting veganism as simply a privileged white phenomenon. If we are to treat veganism as an issue of social justice, and advocate for equality among human and nonhuman animals, our advocacy should especially include other humans who are marginalized and treated as "less than."

There is a segment of the animal advocacy world that is extremely hostile to pro-intersectional vegan advocacy. Some vegans make comments such as, "I hate all humans equally and would love nothing more than to see them all die," and, "Screw those earthquake victims; all of those savages probably ate animals." Not only does the notion of accepting violence of others directly contradict the vegan ethic of standing up to injustice, but it is also an ineffective strategy to help nonhuman animals. If we want the dominant society to develop greater regard for the ongoing injustice that nonhuman animals experience, we need to create a world that is sensitive to injustice and oppression in general.

When we promote hatred and violence in our own language and behavior, we create a world with more hatred and violence, not only towards other humans, but towards all of the inhabitants of our planet. It is also simply not enough to promote justice for non-human animals and express indifference to various forms of human oppression and discrimination. Remaining unconcerned about or disinterested in the injustice that human animals experience while opposing speciesism on the basis of social justice considerations, is morally inconsistent.

I do understand resistance to pro-intersectional advocacy beyond the fact that we collectively do not want to relinquish our privilege. Some fear that they are simply not able to choose their words correctly or to respond in ways that will not offend others. There is some truth in such fears. Pro-intersectional advocacy is not easy and does not necessarily come naturally.

It is something that we need to work on and continuously learn from others, particularly those who experience multiple layers of reciprocating oppression. What is most important, however, is to really focus on listening to those from marginalized groups, and to not attempt to speak over them or tell them that their experiences are not real or legitimate. It is best to maintain a listening mindset while acknowledging that we may make mistakes as we attempt to become better advocates for both human and nonhuman animals.

What if all of the human and economic resources poured into fighting the various forms of injustice were pooled to fight the roots of all injustice? What if everyone who had an interest in social justice recognized that all injustice must be challenged, and worked hard to understand the perspectives of all marginalized and oppressed individuals, human and nonhuman? What if we focused on all of the positive contributions that a truly diverse movement could bring to ending the suffering of all sentient beings? I daresay that this planet and all life forms that inhabit it would be in much better health right now.

CHAPTER 12

TRAUMA IN ANIMAL ADVOCACY

Trauma in animal advocacy is not a topic that one sees discussed very often, but trauma is a central consideration in animal advocacy for a couple of reasons. Many animal advocates have personally experienced trauma themselves. In fact, for many of us, our personal experiences of abuse and injustice are what have helped us develop the mindset that we must fight to prevent all vulnerable creatures from experiencing unnecessary trauma and abuse. When one experiences trauma and abuse, they are more likely to be sensitive to trauma experienced by others and fight for justice for those oppressed.

While the experience of trauma may make us more attuned to the abuse of others, it also may leave us more vulnerable to trauma-related problems such as posttraumatic stress disorder, depression, and substance use difficulties. As animal advocates, we bear witness to extreme atrocities that nonhuman animals experience, some of us on a daily basis. This trauma exposure can wear on us and negatively impact our overall sense of well-being. Some may cope with these problems by turning their frustration and depression outward, resulting in difficulties with anger and aggression. Others may drink or use other substances to try to numb themselves to the pain.

It is important for all of us to be aware of what's going on with us internally, and to decide for ourselves what degree of trauma exposure, if any, we are able to withstand. It does the animals no good if we are incapacitated with sadness and grief as we are exposed to trauma inflicted on them. We all must learn how best to take care of ourselves, both physically and emotionally, and surround ourselves with a supportive network that we can reach out to when we feel sad, frustrated, or a range of other negative emotions. We care so much about these animals and want to end their trauma, but the fact that we can only do so much to immediately end this trauma is devastating to many of us.

I have published research studies based on samples of military Veterans showing that when one experiences trauma, they're more likely to view the world through an overly hostile lens.[23] Some of my research shows that when one is exposed to trauma and experiences posttraumatic stress disorder, they have greater difficulties managing anger, are more likely to interpret events in a negative manner, and are more likely to lash out at others. This is based on a trauma-informed social information-processing model that my colleagues and I have elaborated in recent work.[52]

I mention this because it's important that animal advocates exposed to constant trauma always be mindful that it's easy to go down that abyss and view the world and all of its inhabitants as horrible. While the reality is that there is immense unnecessary suffering and humans are an incredibly destructive species, we need to prevent ourselves from developing such a cynical view that we're not able to effect any kind of change.

In the last chapter we discussed core themes and how they can guide our behavior. Much of my clinical work has focused on how core themes can be disrupted by trauma, which can in turn negatively impact our relationships and ability to communicate. When we experience trauma, it can shake the very foundations of our beliefs and effects can reverberate across several domains of our lives. One of my mentors, Dr. Patricia Resick, developed and tested a highly successful treatment of posttraumatic stress disorder that has consistently and impressively demonstrated that when we address disruptions in these core beliefs, or cognitive schemas, we can help resolve traumas and develop healthier ways of viewing ourselves and others.[53]

For example, when somebody is victimized in some way, or witnesses others being victimized, they may find it difficult to trust others. Or perhaps they suffer from difficulties related to self-esteem. They may harshly judge themselves when they make mistakes or for other minor infractions. Difficulties with trust and self-esteem can lead to depression, anger, and aggressive behavior. Traumatic events involving other people may also lead one to believe that others are not good or don't need to be respected. They may have generalized this belief to everyone, which may also lead to a host of difficulties.

Power and control difficulties can develop when activists feel completely powerless to end horrific animal abuse. A profound sense of helplessness and uncontrollability can lead to chronic feelings of hopelessness. Feelings of powerlessness not only contribute to posttraumatic stress disorder,[54] but they can also contribute to power struggles with others and aggressive interactions.[55]

We can't help others go vegan if we're constantly skeptical of them and we assume the worst about them. We can't help others go vegan if we jump down their throat immediately when they present us with one of the common justifications for animal use that we're all too familiar with. Our best hope of creating a vegan world is to be calm but impassioned, assertive activists who can show non-vegans that we're fully rational, compassionate people who want to help animals and prevent needless violence and abuse.

I have worked with many angry, violent Veterans who experienced severe combat-related trauma and posttraumatic stress disorder who were still able to change their perspective. It is by no means an easy task, but if one really pays close attention to their thoughts and how they are interpreting situations and themselves, as well as their feelings and other signs their bodies give them, they can train themselves to assume the best in others rather than assuming the worst. If we're able to see things without assuming the worst, we're more likely to recognize a desire to change and hints that a non-vegan is open to our vegan message.

We will miss those openings if we're stuck in a state of negativity and hopelessness, so we must find a way to get help if we need it. I encourage anyone struggling with these issues to consider seeing a counselor who specialized in cognitive-behavioral therapy, which has been shown time and time again to be the most effective treatment for trauma-related problems.[56]

Finally, recognizing the trauma experiences of non-vegans may also help open the door for true change to occur. When one experiences trauma, they will be particularly negatively reactive against more aggressive ways of approaching them. I have found that when I hear the person out and let them talk about their experiences, they will be much more likely to listen to my (vegan) point of view. Those who have experienced trauma in particular will be highly resistant to more confrontational, aggressive approaches, which is just another reason to be assertive, not aggressive, in our advocacy (see Chapter 8).

Case Example

Charles is a thirty-five-year old gay, black, vegan man. Growing up as a child, he was regularly beaten by his father, who called him a "faggot" on a daily basis. He was also teased at school for being "different" than the other kids, and he twice attempted suicide. Charles left his family at the age of fifteen to live with his aunt and uncle, and then got his own place when he was eighteen and went vegan soon after. He has since been in two long-term abusive relationships. He mostly keeps to himself because he has a difficult time being around people. He doesn't feel like he can trust anyone, stemming from all of the abuse he's experienced over the course of his life. As far as Charles is concerned, everyone is an abuser and no relationship is safe. He keeps his veganism mostly to himself because he finds that people don't understand it and he doesn't have the patience to try to explain it to them. Frequently when he's exposed to animal cruelty, such as on his Facebook newsfeed, it brings back memories of his own past abuse that also triggers nightmares and flashbacks. Lately he's been living a reclusive life and keeps mostly to himself.

Charles is displaying some of the classic symptoms of posttraumatic stress disorder resulting from his exposure to trauma, such as nightmares, flashbacks, and social isolation. It would be a good idea for him to seek an evaluation with a mental health expert and possibly seek treatment. Finding ways to become more active in the pro-intersectional vegan community, and developing a larger social support network, may also be indicated, as social support is an important buffer of the negative impacts of trauma. This is likely very difficult for Charles due to his trouble trusting others, but at the same time may be what he needs most—to develop social interaction and learn that there are some people out there whom he can learn to trust. He may also become a more assertive animal advocate in the process.

CHAPTER 13

COMMUNICATING WITH NON-VEGAN FRIENDS AND OTHER LOVED ONES

Compounding possible trauma-related issues is the reaction that many vegans receive from the non-vegans around them. It is difficult enough to be regularly exposed to trauma that nonhuman animals may experience; it becomes even more of a struggle for some when those whom we rely upon for support are not supportive regarding this issue. This has implications not only for our own personal well-being and ability to be effective advocates for animals, but also impacts our advocacy directly because we may have the greatest impact in our communication with those whom we are closest to.

I regularly receive emails from recently transitioning vegans or those who desire to go vegan about struggles that they experience with friends and loved ones. Often these messages are from those whose loved ones refuse to accept their veganism. Here's an (adapted) example I email I received:

Hi, Vegan Publishers! I was wondering if you could direct me to some books, resources, or websites that can help me deal with the frustration, anxiety, and anger that I'm feeling as a new vegan. I have been a vegetarian for a long time but transitioned to veganism about five months ago and the response of those around me has been horrific. I naively thought that they'd all be understanding and would be supportive of my efforts to lead a kinder and more compassionate life. That couldn't be further from the truth! They constantly bombard me with all kinds of reasons for why I should give up veganism, and they make fun of my veganism all of the time. I feel like I'm being bullied.

I've been feeling really hopeless lately and haven't wanted anything to do with my old friends and even my family. I thought that if I just explained why I wanted to go vegan to people that they would understand. I plan on being vegan for life because I am too aware of what is done to animals in these cruel industries and I realize that I don't need to be contributing to it. But I also feel all alone here, and I need to find a way to adjust my attitude so I can better deal with social situations or discussions with non-vegans, some of whom are really hostile to my new lifestyle. Your page is incredibly encouraging and makes me feel reassured that there are like-minded people out there!

We should always be mindful that while we have cognitively eliminated the learned false distinctions between different sentient beings, those all around us have not, and therefore they really do not truly understand our perspective. The only way for them to know is for us to be clear in our communication with them and letting them in on how we are changing and what we have learned. Some will not want to know, and there is nothing we can do about that. Others may have real interest, though, which can provide us with an important opportunity to talk about our advocacy and seek support in others.

It is difficult to avoid feeling disappointed when others we are close with do not seem interested in learning more about why we have decided to help nonhuman animals. We may know our loved one as an otherwise compassionate and kind individual, but yet they have closed the door to communicating about the atrocities that are visited upon animals—atrocities that they fund through their purchases and behavior.

The animal advocate may also feel some degree of rejection by loved ones because if they truly sought to understand why we chose to go vegan and speak out for animals, they would naturally join us because there is no logical or ethical justification for the needless killing of animals. This may be the hardest pill of all to swallow; the advocate wants so much for their loved ones to understand their compassion for animals, because it is a huge part of who they are as a person.

Becoming an animal advocate can be especially difficult for those who do not have a large support system. The advocate may remember fondly earlier times when they would confide in their loved ones and share the ways in which they have changed, or what they have learned while living separate-but-connected lives. That may not be possible when one becomes an animal advocate and goes vegan, since many do not want to hear about how we have developed greater compassion for animals and a desire to promote justice for them.

Many vegan advocates are partnered with non-vegans, which can create a great deal of stress on the relationship. Some advocates have gone vegan and became advocates after they were married, and the differences between the couple have become greater and greater over time. Whereas they were at one point on the same page when it came to animal use, now there is a great divide, with one member of the couple engaging in the very behavior that the other member of the couple is fighting against. Some advocates describe having found an agreement with their partners that seems to work for them, while others describe feeling like they no longer share the same values.

In Chapter 8, I discussed the importance of assertive vegan communication. Assertiveness is such a critical skill when communicating with our loved ones because it can help us get our point across while not holding in our feelings or blowing up at others. Setting limits and boundaries is an important component of being assertive. This may involve letting others know what we are willing to accept and not accept.

For example, we may need to let a close friend know that if they continue to engage in bullying behavior surrounding veganism, we will no longer spend time with them. Or being assertive may involve letting family members know that we do not feel comfortable attending a family holiday party if animals will be eaten there. Perhaps we feel like this would be too upsetting to us personally or it may damage our relationship with our family if we witness them cooking and eating animals. We need to be aware of our own needs and feelings and express them in such a way that we are respecting the other person but also our own feelings and beliefs.

Letting others understand our limits and boundaries may also involve the painful process of ending relationships altogether. For animal advocates partnered with non-advocates, they may ultimately need to let their partners know that they can no longer remain with a partner who contributes to the direct harm of animals. While some would argue that couples should remain together at all costs and honor their vows to one another, nobody should remain in a relationship that is doing damage to them emotionally. Unhealthy patterns may develop in these relationships that may ultimately be overcome, or perhaps the differences are too great and reconciliation is no longer an option.

It can also be helpful to always remember that there are no right or wrong feelings, and how one handles a difficult situation with loved ones may work better for them, while a completely different approach would work better for someone else. We can't make one-size-fits-all statements about how we should be managing a difficult situation or communicating with someone whom we care about. There are too many individual and situational variables that come into play to make blanket suggestions for a given situation. The most important point is to always listen to other person, to express oneself to others in as clear a manner as possible, and to not keep feelings in, while being respectful of the other.

It may be helpful to recognize that the longer one advocates for animals, the more they will know, and the better they will be able to respond to challenging situations. Even myself, as a clinical psychologist and communication skills expert, had difficulties in communication with family members when I first went vegan. I did not have ready responses to many of the justifications others used for the mistreatment of nonhuman animals, and as a result I responded more out of frustration and not always in an effective and compassionate manner. After engaging in animal advocacy for a longer period of time, there are few if any arguments or attacks that I may encounter that I have not heard before, and it just becomes quite easy to respond to anything that might come my way, which naturally lessens my anger and frustration.

I believe that the same is true for others. There is no valid ethical or scientific argument in favor of breeding and killing animals, or otherwise using them for our selfish purposes, so we are aided by the fact that the truth is on our side. This should provide us some comfort. When we develop more command over all of the information that is out there regarding our use of animals, we feel less defensive and more confident in discussing the ethics of animal use and our reasons for being animal advocates.

For any successful relationship, there needs to be a balance of working to accept what we can accept about the other person, while also working to change what we can change. Acceptance and change are the cornerstones for some of the most effective therapy approaches for couples and family members.[1] To have continued positive relationships with non-vegan loved ones, the animal advocate may need to continually work to accept that the other person may not change, at least in the short-term. For some of the most influential and highly regarded animal advocates I know, communicating with loved ones about animal use was a long, ongoing process that ultimately led to positive change in some cases, but there are no guarantees. While we never should accept the exploitation of animals as morally defensible, it is entirely up to us whether we continue to accept the non-vegan loved ones into our lives.

CHAPTER 14

OTHER THERAPEUTIC FACTORS

My personal favorite mode of conducing therapy is via groups because if one can marshal all of the resources that the group has to offer, it can be much more powerful than counseling others one-on-one. I have often noted how social media is somewhat like a large group counseling session. The feedback that others on our forum provide to prospective vegans is often much more powerful than what I could offer. When we have a large collective group with one goal in mind—promoting veganism—we can be incredibly effective. It helps when we have a diverse, international following of individuals who can relate to different non-vegans on multiple levels. So I feel that part of my role as a manager of a large social media page is to facilitate positive dialogue and to ensure that discussions go in a positive direction.

Irvin Yalom is considered the master of group therapy, and his groundbreaking book[1] has been considered the gold standard guide for this mode of intervention. Yalom discussed how the group experience is thought to exert a therapeutic effect as a result of a number of primary factors. Detailed discussion of these factors is available in the original source work. I will provide a brief discussion of just some of the key variables below, as it applies to animal advocacy:

1. *Instillation of hope* is very important for any behavioral change effort, as many who are stuck in old patterns may have difficulty finding their way out. Frequently, non-vegans will tell us that they simply don't think that they'd be able to live vegan even though they really want to make the change. They may have difficulty envisioning what their lives would be like if they weren't able to eat their

favorite foods, enjoy the holidays in exactly the same way, and so on.

It is important that the animal advocate consistently communicate hopefulness and optimism, at times explicitly, but more often implicitly, by reflecting upon the non-vegan's desire for changing their animal use patterns, by identifying their strengths and positive gains made, and by nurturing a hopeful, change-oriented atmosphere. This involves believing in the power of these individuals to alter their lives rather than the power of their cravings for animal products.

2. *Universality* of experience, and group identification, is also critical. Those interested in going vegan may feel that they're the "only ones" who care about animals and may feel that they can't make the transition if they have nobody else to help them through. This is why it's so important for transitioning and new vegans, and even longtime vegans, to reach out to available social support networks such as local vegan meet ups, vegan societies, etc. If there is nothing local, there are numerous Facebook pages and groups for vegans, including newly transitioning vegans. There are pages for those with vegan pets, vegans of color, vegan humor, vegan philosophy, pro-intersectional vegans, vegan advocacy, and the list goes on. It's very important for us all to develop our own sense of community, especially when we feel isolated or are transitioning and need help and support more than ever.

3. *Imparting information* can occur in many overt and subtle ways. We as advocates should have as many resources at our fingertips as we can. It's especially helpful to be able to provide this vegan information to those who are in the preparation or action stages of change, since they've made the decision to change but may not yet know how to go about it. This information can involve tangible resources such as advice about shopping and being vegan on a budget, as well as more ethical or spiritual resources that may entail continued discussions of moral questions that may come up.

4. *Altruism* in reference to vegans and aspiring vegans is providing one another with help and support. This is a powerful element in any context with multiple individuals that we should consistently model and encourage. There is no greater or more profound feeling than knowing that we've helped someone make a lifelong change and end their support of the needless suffering of nonhuman animals while asking for nothing in return.

5. *Imitative behavior*, or observational learning, is another powerful way to promote change in others. Those who are vegan or simply further along the stages of change can serve as role models for curious and aspiring vegans. When we speak out for animals it only makes it easier for others to do the same. This is why it's so critical to not only live vegan, but to also serve as a role model for how we can openly advocate for other animals. Showing that we live as happy, healthy vegans demonstrates some of the great side benefits of going vegan, such as improved

health and spiritual well-being. Non-vegans will be most likely to "imitate" or learn from others who are having success in their vegan transition.

6. *Catharsis* refers simply to the expression of emotion, both good and bad. Often this refers to emotions that have not been formerly expressed, or perhaps not even clearly labeled or experienced. This is why I think it's important to not only try to message to non-vegans, but also other vegans who may be having difficulty in dealing with non-vegan loved ones or others. Even long-time vegans need opportunities to "vent" their frustrations and discuss their feelings with like-minded individuals who understand what they're going through.

7. *Existential factors* refers to the sense of purpose or meaning in life, which cannot simply be conjured up or artificially derived. The sense of meaning is most likely to emerge from deep engagement with something outside of one's self. Veganism offers an opportunity to focus very deeply on others' pain, struggles, and joy in a way that may have been formerly unavailable in their everyday life. An important sense of meaning can result from these experiences.

The following adapted thread taken from our Vegan Publishers Facebook page illustrates each of these therapeutic factors described in this chapter:

Yolanda: I'm almost 100% vegan now! I've almost cut out all meat except for some chicken but am slowly giving that up too. I feel better than ever physically and my body is thanking me for it.

CT: That's great, Yolanda! How can we help you take the final step to going vegan? Gardein vegan chicken tastes exactly like the animal versions.

Yolanda: You've already helped me decide to go vegan the last time I emailed you, and you suggested cookbooks that were really useful. I haven't had any chicken since the last time we wrote on here a few weeks ago so things are going great now.

Jennifer: Yolanda, it sounds like you're ready to just kick it! If you think you feel good now, just wait until you take that final step.

Yolanda: Tell me about it. I'm really excited! I just have to start trying new vegan foods now.

CT: Yay!

Jennifer: You will find a ton of vegan recipes online. If you have any questions, feel free to ask or private message me.

Susan: Thank you for going vegan, Yolanda!

Nancy: There are some great tasting vegan mock chicken products on the market. Give them a shot.

Barbara: My personal favorite is Gardein! They should have them at your local health food store and even most big box stores. You can even get a holiday roast for the holidays!

Tara: I'm slowly getting there too. I've removed beef and pork from my diet and am trying to eat more alkaline foods. I eventually will be fully vegan.

CT: Good for you, Tara!

Tara: If anyone has good recipes for me, let me know.

Patrick: Check this link for this vegan sandwich recipe, Tara, it's amazing! [provides link]

Mindy: Way to go, Yolanda and Tara! Both of you can do it!

Tara: Thanks for the recipe, Patrick. I love sundried tomatoes and chickpeas—this looks really yummy.

Kelly: I have been vegetarian for over twenty years but now am ready to try going vegan. My downfall has always been cheese. What are some good replacements for dairy cheese?

Sarah: Kelly, check out the movie *Earthlings*. It will help you go fully vegan. I also had some trouble kicking the cheese (and ice cream) habit until I watched that, but haven't touched the stuff ever since.

CT: Kelly, there are some great vegan cheeses out there. Chao cheese is all the rage now. It tastes just like dairy cheese. There are also some great nut-based cheeses. The truth is that after about a month or so without eating dairy, you won't even miss it. The longer you go without it, the less you will crave it.

Koby: I am really grateful for how nice everyone is here and how they don't hate some of us for not yet being vegan, but encourage us to get there! I believe that we all can do it! For me, I live with my parents and they won't let me go vegan, just vegetarian. I plan to go vegan as soon as I move out. My parents make me eat dairy, but I don't eat meat and don't support any other kind of animal exploitation, such as leather or zoos. My eczema has gotten worse since I've gone vegetarian, though. Does anybody know if dairy could be the cause of that?

Barbara: Koby, here's a good link for that! [provides link]

This thread is a great example of how powerful these therapeutic factors can be. Note the great mix between instilling hope and providing support with the provision of more tangible resources. Creating a safe space for aspiring vegans, new vegans, and long-time vegans to openly discuss how to overcome barriers to going vegan and to develop bonds with one another over the issue of veganism is conducive to an atmosphere that ultimately produces a high likelihood for significant behavioral change.

CHAPTER 15

CONCLUSIONS

I have kept the discussion focused on some specific areas in which clinical psychology and interventions designed to enhance motivation for changing problematic behavior can help inform our advocacy. In short, we should be aware of a person's barriers to going vegan and should work to build an alliance with them while maintaining a clear position regarding the ethics of animal use and veganism and also remaining aware of the individual's current level of motivation for change. We should also take care to use language that will be the most compelling and doesn't put others on the defensive or induce shame in them, or cause them to feel unsafe, because this will cause them to shut down and stop listening. It is most helpful to put out a variety of messages, since no singular message will be effective for everyone because each individual may be in a different stage of change than the next. However, we must always emphasize veganism as the end goal to strive for if we view it as a social justice issue and hope to help others go vegan. It just makes sense that if we want people to go vegan, we cannot be afraid of promoting veganism! Finally, I discussed the importance of pro-intersectionality, since various forms of injustice are all connected via common causes, or core themes. It is my sincere hope that we all continue to work hard at fighting injustice in all forms. The health and well-being of our planet and future generations depend on it.

I implore all animal advocates to always remain mindful of your own psychological state. The challenges we face are truly daunting, and we will be in this fight for our entire lives. We have enormous financial, political, and cognitive barriers against effecting the massive change that is needed to end the devastation of sentient life and our planet in general. When we bear witness to the atrocities nonhuman animals are exposed to, and the indifference and downright hostility that many express to those trying to help animals, it can be traumatizing and disheartening to say the least. We need to make sure that we are taking proper care of ourselves mentally and physically so that we can keep fighting for the animals in a positive way.

Although it can be easy to focus on the barriers and the challenges, it is clear that change is happening. The younger generation is much more likely to be vegan than previous generations, the food industry is increasingly going more vegan, and the fast food chains that have historically been the biggest killers of animals have been struggling mightily.[1] I receive emails almost every day from young people who are asking for help in going vegan, or who simply want more information. This is new. Things are changing at an accelerated pace. With the expansion of social media, there is no longer an ironclad way to keep the horrors of animal agriculture hidden, and the general public is being made aware of the harm done to those all around us. So now more than ever, we need to keep up the fight because the animals deserve nothing less.

There is so much new energy flowing into the animal advocacy movement right now and it is critically important that our efforts are focused. If we can help teach young people that our animal use is truly a social injustice, and encourage them to go vegan and to help others go vegan, we will have made the best possible use of this amazing energy that we possibly can. If we teach them that it is okay to abuse animals in moderation, they will then work against the efforts of those who are doing great vegan education work. We need to be thoughtful as advocates and avoid giving conflicting messages and causing the efforts of some to cancel out the efforts of others. We need to do better than that, and I believe that we will in the not too distant future.

Whether or not the animal advocacy movement is successful really depends on the people at the grassroots level. I do not believe that the large animal advocacy groups will ultimately be responsible for an end to all animal use, not only because they refuse to unequivocally promote veganism and treat it as an issue of social justice, but also because they do not really reflect the diversity of the people and skill sets that they possess.

We will truly have a vegan world when people from all backgrounds and walks of life make the decision to offer their very best efforts and skill sets towards ending our animal use. This will involve doctors talking to their patients not only about vegan nutrition, but also about the ethics of our animal use. This will involve conversations around the dinner table with loved ones, discussions at school board meetings, conversations with our local mechanics, barbers, politicians, etc. This will involve lawyers, researchers, marketers, behavioral change experts, and professionals from all walks of life donating their time and effort to ending animal use and abuse.

For these kinds of education efforts to truly have an impact and help create a vegan world, of course they need to focus on actual veganism and a discussion of ethics. Treating veganism as a diet or as a health issue is not going to change our current systems of animal oppression. We need society to increase its level of awareness and consciousness about animal use just as we vegans have done on a personal level. We will not trick others to become more aware of systematic animal abuse; we have to teach them about it and encourage them to teach others. That is truly the only way we will find our way out of this mess collectively and begin to help heal the trauma that we have inflicted upon ourselves, other sentient animals, and the planet.

NOTES

Chapter 1: Introduction

1. Cooney, N. (2010). *Change of Heart: What Psychology Can Teach Us About Spreading Social Change*. Lantern Books.
2. Cooney, N. (2014). *Veganomics: The Surprising Science on What Motivates Vegetarians, from the Breakfast Table to the Bedroom*. Lantern Books.
3. Francione, G. L. & Charlton, A. (2015). *Animal Rights: The Abolitionist Approach*. Exempla Press.
4. Francione, G. L. (2010). *The Animal Rights Debate: Abolition or Regulation?* Columbia University Press.

Chapter 2: Promoting Change in the Context of Social Justice

1. The Vegan Society. (2014). "Ripened by human determination: 70 Years of The Vegan Society." http://www.vegansociety.com/sites/default/files/uploads/Ripened%20by%20human%20determination.pdf.
2. Francione, G. L. *Animal Rights*.
3. Leenaert, T. (2015). "The fetish of being vegan." http://veganstrategist.org/tag/communication/.
4. Oliver, H. (2015). "The Leader of the New 'Reducetarian Movement Questions the Morality of Eating Meat." https://www.vice.com/read/the-leader-of-the-reducetarian-movement-reckons-we-should-all-eat-less-meat-2.

Chapter 3: Language Is Important

1. Patrick-Goudreau, C. (2011). *Vegan's Daily Companion: 365 Days of Inspiration for Cooking, Eating, and Living Compassionately*. Beverly, MA: Quarry Books.
2. Cooney, N. *Veganomics*.

Chapter 4: What Does the Science Tell Us About Effective Animal Advocacy?

1. Wrenn, C. (2015). *A Rational Approach to Animal Rights: Extensions in Abolitionist Theory*. Palgrave Macmillan.
2. Humane Research Council. (December 2014). "Study of Current and Former Vegetarians and Vegans." https://faunalytics.org/wp-content/uploads/2015/06/Faunalytics_Current-Former-Vegetarians_Full-Report.pdf.
3. Doebel, S., Gabriel, S., & The Humane League. (August 2015). "Report: Does Encouraging The Public To 'Eat Vegan,' 'Eat Vegetarian,' 'Eat Less Meat,' or 'Cut Or Cut Back On' Meat And Other Animal Products Lead To The Most Diet Change?" Humane League Labs. https://humaneleaguelabs.files.wordpress.com/2015/09/humane-league-labs-best-request.pdf.

4. Wikipedia (2016). "Pseudoscience." https://en.wikipedia.org/wiki/Pseudoscience.
5. Cooney, N. *Change of Heart.*
6. Cooney, N. *Veganomics.*
7. Cialdini, R. B. (2006). *Influence: The Psychology of Persuasion, Revised Edition.* Harper Business.
8. Taft, C. T., Macdonald, A., Creech, S. K., Monson, C. M., & Murphy, C. M. (2015). "A randomized controlled trial of the Strength at Home Men's Program for Partner Violence in Military Veterans." *Journal of Clinical Psychiatry.*
9. Hayes, M. A., Gallagher, M. W., Gilbert, K. S., Creech, S. K., DeCandia, C. J., Beach, C. A., & Taft, C. T. (2015). "Targeting relational aggression in Veterans: The Strength at Home friends and family intervention." *Journal of Clinical Psychiatry,* 76(6), 774–778.

Chapter 5: Why Do People Continue to Live Non-Vegan?

1. Joy, M. (2011). *Why We Love Dogs, Eat Pigs, and Wear Cows: An Introduction to Carnism.* Conari Press.
2. Lawrence, A. E., & Taft, C. T. (2013). "Shame, posttraumatic stress disorder, and intimate partner violence perpetration." *Aggression and Violent Behavior,* 18, 191-194.
3. Free From Harm. (2014). "Eating Animals: Addressing Our Most Common Justifications." http://freefromharm.org/eating-animals-addressing-our-most-common-justifications/.
4. Francione, G. L. (2013). *Eat Like You Care: An Examination of the Morality of Eating Animals.* CreateSpace Independent Publishing Platform.
5. Eisman, G. (2015). *A Guide to Vegan Nutrition.* Vegan Publishers.
6. Taft, C. T., A randomized controlled trial.
7. McFall R. M. (1982). "A review and reformulation of the concept of social skills." *Behavioral Assessment,* 4(1):1–33.
8. Anglin, K., & Holtzworth-Munroe, A. (1997). "Comparing the responses of maritally violent and nonviolent spouses to problematic marital and nonmarital situations: Are the skill deficits of physically aggressive husbands and wives global?" *Journal of Family Psychology,* 11, 301-313. doi: 10.1037/0893-3200.11.3.301.
9. Eckhardt, C. I., Barbour, K. A., & Davison, G. C. (1998). "Articulated thoughts of maritally violent and nonviolent men during anger arousal." *Journal of Consulting and Clinical Psychology,* 66, 259-269. doi: 10.1037/0022-006X.66.2.259.
10. Eckhardt, C. I., & Jamison, T. R. (2002). "Articulated thoughts of male perpetrators of dating violence during anger arousal." *Cognitive Therapy and Research,* 26, 289–308. doi: 10.1023/A:1016045226185.

11. Eckhardt, C. I., & Kassinove, H. (1998). "Articulated cognitive distortions and cognitive deficiencies in maritally violent men." *Journal of Cognitive Psychotherapy*, 12, 231-250. Retrieved from http://www.springerpub.com/journal-of-cognitive-psychotherapy.html.

12. Taft, C. T., Weatherill, R. P., Panuzio Scott, J., Thomas, S. A., Kang, H. K., & Eckhardt, C. I. (2015). "Social information processing in anger expression and partner violence in returning Veterans." *Journal of Traumatic Stress, 28*, 314–321.

Chapter 6: Long-Term Goal Setting

1. Mitchell, T., & Daniels, D. (2003). "Motivation" in W. Borman, D. Ilgen, J. Klimoski (Eds.), *Comprehensive Handbook of Psychology: Industrial Organizational Psychology* (Vol. 12, 225–254). New York, NY: Wiley.

2. Locke, E., & Latham, G. (1990). *A Theory of Goal Setting and Task Performance.* Englewood Cliffs, NJ: Prentice Hall.

3. Locke, E. A., & Latham, G. P. (2002). "Building a practically useful theory of goal setting and task motivation. A 35-year odyssey." *American Psychologist*, 57, 705–717. http://dx.doi.org/10.1037/0003-066X.57.9.705.

4. Kanfer, R. (1990). "Motivation theory and industrial and organizational psychology" in M. D. Dunnette & L. M. Hough (Eds.), *Handbook of Industrial and Organizational Psychology* (2nd ed., vol. 1, 75–170). Palo Alto, CA: Consulting Psychologists Press.

5. Locke, E. *A Theory of Goal Setting.*

Chapter 7: Relationships in Vegan Advocacy

1. Krupnick, J. L., Sotsky, S. M., Simmens, S., Moyer, J., Elkin, I., Watkins, J., & Pilkonis, P. A. (1996). "The role of the therapeutic alliance in psychotherapy and pharmacotherapy outcome: Findings in the National Institute of Mental Health Treatment of Depression Collaborative Research Program." *Journal of Consulting and Clinical Psychology*, 64, 532–539.

2. Taft, C. T., Murphy, C. M., King, D. W., Musser, P. H., & DeDeyn, J. M. (2003). "Process and treatment adherence factors in group cognitive-behavioral therapy for partner violent men." *Journal of Consulting and Clinical Psychology, 71(4),* 812–820.

3. Taft, C. T., & Murphy, C. M. (2007). "The working alliance in intervention for partner violence perpetrators: Recent research and theory." *Journal of Family Violence, 22,* 11–18.

4. Markman, H. J., Stanley, S. M., & Blumberg, S. L. (2010). *Fighting for Your Marriage: A Deluxe Revised Edition of the Classic Best-Seller for Enhancing Marriage and Preventing Divorce.* Jossey-Bass.

Chapter 8: Assertive Vegan Communication
1. Linehan, M. M., & Egan, K. J. (1979). "Assertion training for women" in A. S. Bellack & M. Hersen (Eds.), *Research and Practice in Social Skills Training* (237–271). New York: Plenum Press.

Chapter 9: The Stages of Intentional Behavioral Change
1. Prochaska, J. and DiClemente, C. (1983) "Stages and processes of self-change in smoking: toward an integrative model of change." *Journal of Consulting and Clinical Psychology*, 5, 390.
2. Miller, W. R., & Rollnick, S. (2012). *Motivational Interviewing: Helping People Change, 3rd Edition.* The Guilford Press.
3. VanBuskirk, K. A., & Wetherell, J. L. (2014). "Motivational interviewing with primary care populations: A systematic review and meta-analysis." *Journal of Behavioral Medicine*, 37(4), 768–780.
4. Free From Harm. "Eating Animals."
5. Francione, G. L. *Eat Like You Care.*
6. Magill, M., Gaume, J., Apodaca, T. R., Walthers, J., Mastroleo, N. R., Borsari, B., & Longabaugh, R. (2014). "The technical hypothesis of motivational interviewing: A meta-analysis of MI's key causal model." *Journal of Consulting and Clinical Psychology*, 82(6), 973–983.
7. Mangels, R. (2011). *The Everything Vegan Pregnancy Book: All You Need to Know for a Healthy Pregnancy that Fits Your Lifestyle.* Adams Media.
8. Miller, W. R., & Rose, G. S. (2015). "Motivational interviewing and decisional balance: Contrasting responses to client ambivalence." *Behavioural and Cognitive Psychotherapy*, Vol. 43(2), 129–141.

Chapter 11: Targeting Core Themes
1. The Curvy Vegan (2014). "Angela Davis: Why Being Vegan is a Part of a Revolutionary Perspective." http://www.thecurvyvegan.com/angela-davis-vegan.html.
2. Tuttle, W. (Ed.). (2014). *Circles of Compassion: Connecting Issues of Justice.* Vegan Publishers.
3. Crenshaw, K. (1989). "Demarginalizing the Intersection of Race and Sex: A Black Feminist Critique of Antidiscrimination Doctrine, Feminist Theory and Antiracist Politics." *The University of Chicago Legal Forum* 140: 139–167.
4. Knudsen, S. V. (2006). "Intersectionality – A Theoretical Inspiration in the Analysis of Minority Cultures and Identities in Textbooks" 61–76 in E. Bruillard, B. Aamotsbakken, S., Knudsen, S. V. and Horsley, M. (eds). *Caught in the Web or Lost in the Textbook?* Caen: IARTEM, Stef, Iufm.

118

5. Crenshaw, K. (1991). "Mapping the margins: Intersectionality, Identity Politics, and Violence against Women of Color." *Stanford Law Review* 43(6):1241–1299.

6. Jones, P. (October 11, 2013). "Intersectionality and Animals." *Vine Sanctuary News.*

7. Young, J. E., Klosko, J. S., & Weishaar, M. E. (2006). *Schema Therapy: A Practitioner's Guide.* The Guilford Press.

8. Harris, M., & Fallot, R. (2001). "Using trauma theory to design service systems." *New Directions for Mental Health Services, 89.* Jossey Bass.

9. McJetters, C. S. (2014). "Slavery. It's Still a Thing" in W. Tuttle (Ed.), *Circles of Compassion: Connecting Issues of Justice.* Vegan Publishers.

10. Gendler, S. (2012). "How often do Americans eat vegetarian meals? And how many adults in the U.S. are vegetarian?" *The Vegetarian Research Group Blog.* http://www.vrg.org/blog/2012/05/18/how-often-do-americans-eat-vegetarian-meals-and-how-many-adults-in-the-u-s-are-vegetarian/.

Chapter 12: Trauma in Animal Advocacy

1. Eckhardt, C. I. "Articulated thoughts."

2. Taft, C.T., Murphy, C. M., & Creech, S. K. (in press). "Trauma-Informed Treatment and Prevention of Intimate Partner Violence." *American Psychological Association.*

3. Resick, P. A., & Schnicke, M. K. (1992). "Cognitive processing therapy for sexual assault victims." *Journal of Consulting and Clinical Psychology, 60*(5), 748–756.

4. Finkelhor, D., & Browne, A. (1985). "The traumatic impact of child sexual abuse: A conceptualization." *American Journal of Orthopsychiatry, 55*(4), 530–541.

5. Schwartz, J. P., Waldo, M., & Daniel, D. (2005). "Gender-role conflict and self-esteem: Factors associated with partner abuse in court-referred men." *Psychology of Men & Masculinity, 6*(2), 109–113.

6. Keane, T. M., Marshall, A. D., Taft, C. T. (2006). "Posttraumatic stress disorder: Etiology, epidemiology, and treatment outcome." *Annual Review of Clinical Psychology, 2,* 161–197.

Chapter 13: Communicating with Non-Vegan Friends and Other Loved Ones

1. Christensen, A., & Jacobson, N. S. (1998). *Acceptance and Change in Couple Therapy: A Therapist's Guide to Transforming Relationships.* W.W. Norton and Company (1st edition).

Chapter 14: Other Therapeutic Factors

1. Yalom, I. D. (1995). *The Theory and Practice of Group Psychotherapy*. Basic Books.

Chapter 15: Conclusions

1. Kamila, A. Y. (September 2015). "Millennials lead food industry toward greener territory." Portland Press Herald.